THE
WRONG PATH

PHIL R BRYSON

Copyright © 2019 by Phil R Bryson.

ISBN Softcover   978-1-950580-93-4

All rights reserved. No part of this book may be reproduced or transmitted in any form or by any means, electronic or mechanical, including photocopying, recording, or by any information storage and retrieval system without express written permission from the author, except in the case of brief quotations embodied in critical reviews and certain other non-commercial uses permitted by copyright law.

Printed in the United States of America.

To order additional copies of this book, contact:
Bookwhip
1-855-339-3589
https://www.bookwhip.com

Boom! A cannon shot rang out across the parade ground. I stepped onto the board that had served as my bed, gripped the iron bars framing the window, peered out and watched as the Admiral's Flag was raised. My heart leapt, for this was to be my day.

I stepped down onto the floor and stared out of my cell into the adjoining room of the gatehouse. It was time to put on my best uniform, for today I was to be court-martialled and finally leave the royal navy.

As I stood there wearing my bellbottoms and white front, I pondered about it. Why on earth had I ever joined the royal navy and when had it all started?

CHAPTER ONE

I suppose my yearning to join the royal navy started in my youth. I lived in Hendon and was attending my weekly scout troop meeting, where for a change we were shown a film about life on an aircraft carrier. I thought to myself, *'Wow, that looks good!'* Plus after the film, the scoutmaster announced that one of the older scouts was to join the air force as a pilot. I looked at him and realized I'd seen him before. He was at the same school as me, Hendon Grammar School and was very popular.

A year or so later my parents moved from Hendon to Basildon. Their house was going to be pulled down to make way for the M1 motorway and they were quite fortunate to sell the house before it was bought, under a compulsory purchase order, which meant they would have got less money for it.

When the headmaster, heard about me moving he called me into his office. He was very authoritive and it was with some apprehension that I entered his study.

He looked up from his desk and said, "Good morning Bryson. I hear you are leaving us."

"That's correct sir," I shakily replied.

"May I suggest when you arrive at your new school that you do not go into the top stream, but a lower stream."

"Yes sir," I replied, knowing full well I would do whatever I was asked.

"I notice you took your eleven plus examination in Ealing." "Yes sir."

"Normally, I have a word with optimistic heads I know locally but in this case, as you arrived from another area it was out of my hands. As long as you adhere to what I've said, all will be well."

"Yes sir," I replied and the interview was over. As for the headmaster he didn't think much of my learning abilities.

I was thirteen and at a new school and oddly enough, there were no girls. What's more Barstable the school I was supposed to attend wasn't built and I found myself at Woodlands. I'd been there a few days and a group of us were gathered around in the playground. Someone said, "What shall we call him?"

A quick thinker replied, "He's always smiling. Let's call him Smiler."

The following lesson was physical education and I told the boys, "I've got no kit."

"It doesn't matter," they replied.

So there I was sitting in the changing room and the PE master, handed out paper and the class told me to stand up and as I did they cried out, "New boy, new boy sir!"

The PE Master approached me and said, "And you can wipe that stupid grin off your face, right away!" The class was in hysterics and from that day hence, I never did get on with the PE Master. In fact one year he wrote on my school report, *Thinks he is the class comedian.*

Eventually we moved into Barstable Grammar Technical school and once again I was in the class with girls and believe it or not. I was not in the top class.

Initially I had wanted to join the sea cadets but couldn't find any in Basildon and joined the Air Training Corp, thinking I might be able to learn to fly. I went away to an RAF camp and went flying in a small monoplane and it was amazing. There was just the pilot and me, I sat behind him and we did a bit of hedgehopping, I thoroughly enjoyed it but after that I left the air training corps.

In 1963 I was fifteen and things were really starting to change. There was pirate radio and in the town centre of Basildon there was a Mecca Dancehall, where on a Friday night there would be various bands appearing. These were organised by the apprentices at Marconi and it was good to see bands like The Who, Searchers, and Animals, to name just a few all play live. Plus the local band was the Dave Clark Five.

In 1964 I was a paperboy and also being sixteen asked my parents if I could have a motorbike. They said no as they were too dangerous but as a friend of mum's rode a scooter, this was deemed to be a lot safer and I ended up with a scooter and became a mod. I was the first to arrive at school on a scooter.

I left school with the grand total of two GCEs and by some miracle managed to get a job at Standard Telephones and Cables as an apprentice. Then my parents moved again, this time to Hawkwell in Essex near Southend-on-Sea I would ride my scooter to work in Basildon and being an apprentice didn't do much, this was because for nine weeks at a time I went to Thurrock Technical College in Grays. At college we apprentices from STC joined up with apprentices from other firms to study city and guilds. As we were there on what was termed block release for nine weeks, not only did we study our own subjects, but we also studied metallurgy and there was a recreational type of lesson run by a young avant-garde lecturer and his lessons were so varied that one day we watched a programme about The Good Soldier Schweik and another time the lecturer said, "I have here a test that will define which job you would be best suited for."

Once we'd filled them in and handed them back he said, "This is odd, I've never seen one like this before."

"What does it say?" We asked.

"Well this person should either be a radio engineer or, an entertainer."

"Whose is it?" We asked.

It was mine and the whole class laughingly replied. "Oh yes, Smiler should be an entertainer."

The lecturer said to me, "And what would you like to do?" "I'd like to be a DJ," I replied.

"Well judging from this test that would appear to be the ideal job for you. Good luck."

After work or college of a night I'd ride into Southend and go into one of two coffee bars, either The Capri or Jacobean. Outside there would always be a row of scooters but as the weather got colder the numbers diminished to two scooters, Mick's and mine. We both had Lambrettas but whereas mine was 150cc his was 200cc. I'd enter walk down the wooden stairs stand in a dimly lit narrow passage and queue up at the coffee bar which had Gaggia coffee machines and buy an orange drink for a shilling, about 5p in today's currency, then go down into the basement, which was a large brighter room with seats around the walls, hit the jukebox and loon about. There was always guaranteed to be a good crowd down there. As a mod the music was just so amazing and the sounds that emanated from the jukebox were mind blowing; everything from soul and RnB to bands like the Who and the Small Faces. In fact quite often the 'B' side of a record would get played over and over again. Being a mod there were always girls about and I distinctly remember being in the driveway of a girl I knew, who was with her friend and stood around as I changed a cable on my scooter. They got bored so one of the girls gave me a love bite, but like the love bite and to a certain extent, being a mod, everything was about to change.

As much as I enjoyed being a mod I really wanted to travel. Nowadays everyone does it back then hardly anyone went abroad and so I decide to join the navy. I sent off an application form to join the royal navy and dad said, "Look son, why don't you join the merchant navy?"

I applied to the merchant shipping office in London to become a navigating officer and was sent along to do an eyesight test, which involved being in a dark room where I was shown red, green and two types of white lights; one of the white lights was slightly yellow this apparently represented old oil lights, which were still in use on some ships.

These lights were then flashed up in front of me and I had to shout out the responding colours. Having finished the test the examiner said, "You've made a few mistakes, they're not damning mistakes but they will have to be submitted to the chief examiner."

I returned to the shipping office and told the chap what had happened to which he replied. "You look like a man of the world so I'll be frank with you."

There's me thinking, *me a man of the world and yet I wasn't even eighteen.*

He continued, "Everyone that has been submitted to the chief examiner so far this year has failed. Who knows, perhaps you will be the exception, but then I see you only have two GCE O levels, this means you will also have to take more GCEs and they will have to include maths and physics."

I returned home to Hawkwell and told my parents. When the letter did arrive I'd failed the eyesight test, but was informed I could join Esso as an apprentice engine room officer. To which my dad replied, "You're not doing that, you'll never see the light of day."

I filled in an application form to join the royal navy as an aircraft mechanic and sent it off.

I was back at college and said to the avant-garde lecturer, "I'm going to join the navy."

"Is that the royal or merchant navy?" He asked.

"The royal navy," I eagerly replied.

"You do realise the royal navy is still run by Nelson."

After another nine weeks at college I returned to STC and as it was the second year of my apprenticeship, I was asked to sign my indentures and refused. I'd made up my mind to join the royal navy but this almost caused a strike. This was because the firm were going to sack me but once word got out about my not signing the indentures, nothing else was said.

Eventually I received a reply from the royal navy and they asked me to go for an interview at their local recruiting office. I put on my tab-collared shirt and knitted tie and wore trousers as opposed to my studded Levi jeans (they had metal buttons instead of a zip fly). I entered the office where a man wearing a jacket, shirt and tie said, "May I help you?"

Having informed him of my reason for being there he said, "I would like you to fill out this form. Take your time."

He then perused it saying, "You've put here as likes, girls, riding your scooter and playing the jukebox. May I make a suggestion?"

"Okay," I replied.

"Shall we say you like travelling and listening to music?"

I was then handed another form, this was an aptitude test. Once I'd finished the man checked my answers and said, "You've done quite well, so I'd like to make a suggestion. We are currently recruiting for mechanician apprentices and this means once you've finished your training, you will be a petty officer. How does that sound?"

"Yeh sounds all right."

"Good, the next thing is we will send you to London for a medical and once you pass that as I'm sure that you're fit, you will then be sent to Portsmouth to undergo a series of tests. If all goes well, we will send you your papers to join the navy. You will not have to pay for any of this, as you will be issued with a rail pass to enable you to go to London and, when you go to Portsmouth to undergo tests for a few days this will all be paid for by the navy. You will get free rail travel and you will be put up and fed all at the navy's expense. How does that sound?"

"Sounds ok."

"Good, now as the course for a mechanician is rather long, instead of signing on for nine years and three in reserve, you will have to serve twelve years. Will that be all right?"

"Fine."

"We will write to you with the relevant details." He then shook my hand and said, "Good luck."

I had left the apprenticeship and was working for Southend Corporation as a road labourer. It was a bit of a doddle and paid better than the apprenticeship. Eventually my rail pass and details of where I was to go in London arrived.

I took a day off work and turned up at the recruiting office in Holborn Kingsway, where I was given a medical and told I was fit enough for the navy. This I thought was odd, as I have flat feet but then it occurred to me, the navy don't march, they go around on ships.

Eventually I received the information about the tests to be taken at Portsmouth and I was asked to state the times of the trains I would catch. I was duly informed to catch earlier trains. As the tests were for a few days, I quit my job as a labourer and applied to work in a milk yard.

In Portsmouth I made friends with Bryan, Ian, Bob and a few others. Once the tests were over we went our separate ways and every day I waited to see if I'd passed. Also there were two types of mechanician, weapons and electrical. Dad advised me to go for electrics as weapons, was not very good for promotion. (Dad had served in the Second World War as a wireless operator and served on the Arctic Convoy to Russia).

I had to take a maths test for the job in the milk yard. The job entailed making up the orders for the milkmen. I had to add up the prices in my head and then ensure they were correct by using an adding machine. I could not let an order go, until both answers tallied. I passed and started the following Monday. I got on well with the boss and the milkmen and had I failed to get into the navy, I could probably have made a career out of it. At last my test results arrived. I had passed and was told to report to HMS St Vincent on the 9th May 1966. I gave in my notice at the milk yard and the boss and milkmen were sad to see me go, but they all wished me luck.

I left my parents' house in Hawkwell carrying a case and mum thinking the next time she saw me I would be a petty officer. I reached the end of the cul-de-sac, turned left and wandered past the few shops and up the hill to the White Hart pub and then down the hill to Hockley Station. I was so happy and wondering if I'd see the same blokes as I'd met on the tests.

In those days the carriages were split into compartments with no passageway and seeing an open door I entered the carriage and hoisted my case into the rack above the seats and sat down. My mind was a million miles away thinking about the new life I was due to start. An ex-girlfriend was on the train with her new boyfriend. "Hello Smiler," she said. "Where are you off to?"

"I'm off to do 12 years in the navy," I said with pride. She turned to her new bloke and said, "Ere Ben, why don't you do something stupid like that?"

CHAPTER TWO

At Portsmouth station, I once again met Bryan and Ian. We were like old friends.

I said to Ian, "How come you've got blond hair and dark eyebrows? Are you using an eyebrow pencil?"

"You cheeky git Smiler. What could I expect from you, but it does arouse much suspicion from girls."

"It's good to see you two, I wonder who else we'll see?" asked Bryan, who was about my height and dark haired.

We boarded the ferry for Gosport and headed for H.M.S. St. Vincent where a high brick wall surrounded a parade ground. The far side of the square was dominated by a very tall mast and boy did I have a yearning to climb to the top of it. Behind the mast was a large brick building, this was to be my home for the next few weeks. We were directed to an office had our names ticked off and when they got to Bryan the sailors said, "Ah, we wondered what you'd look like."

This was presumably their attempt at humour, as Bryan's surname was a bit different.

A group of us were taken up to the first floor and shown to a long room on the right of the large brick building. The floor was wooden and highly polished, on either side was a row of beds, by each bed was a square grey locker, higher up throwing light upon the room were large windows which slid up and down and were sectioned into squares.

To fill out the mess us Mech. Apps were billeted with writers (apparently both mechanician apprentices and writers were seen as intelligent ratings) and Ian was nominated as class leader. I also got to know a couple of Manchurians, Greigson who was a tall stocky chap and had at one time been a bouncer and was known as Greg and Lenny who was tall and thin. One of the writers had the most peculiar habit of sleeping with his boots on.

Once we were all assembled in the mess, a slim dark haired Petty Officer (a GI, gunnery instructor) who wore an amazingly shiny pair of boots said, "I'm Petty Officer Brandon and I'll be your instructor for the next six weeks and in that time you will learn the basics of seamanship. While you are here, you are to refer to myself and all other instructors as sir." He pointed to the mess on the other side of the staircase and said, "The mess opposite will be run by Petty Officer Proudman (GI). He and I are rivals, but it appears I have got the better class of recruit and so I want you to beat them at **everything**."

We then marched down to the stores where we were promptly issued with underwear, sheets, blue shirts, dark blue trousers and a belt (which had a useful money pocket in it). These, we were informed, would be our working clothes and would be called Number Eights. We were also handed badges (which depicted our jobs), nametags, shoes and shoe brushes, a kit bag, which was then stamped on the base with our official number. Mine was P/091800. We stowed everything in our kit bags and were finally issued with our names and initials in wood, which were arranged into a block and enabled us to stamp our names on our clothes. There was also a small blue bag, which was laughingly called a Housewife; this contained needles, thread and wool for darning.

Back in the mess, we were told to undress and put on our Eights. All we could keep was our own underwear, but the rest of our clothes were sent home.

We then had to sew on our badges, plus the cap tally, which is the ribbon with the ship's name on it, had to be fitted around the cap, tied in a bow and cut to size. I found it easy to sew on the badges because I'd actually learnt to sew at school.

Over the following weeks we were shown how to neatly lay out our kit on the bed and in the locker and how to make the bed, with envelope corners.

We were also issued with a Number Two uniform this is the uniform most people would recognise a sailor in and consisted of bell-bottoms and an odd top that zipped up and had a collar. When I put it on, the store man said, "There must be something wrong."

"Why?" I asked.

"Because the uniform fits you."

There was also a separate blue collar that had three white lines at its edge, this was a very awkward thing to wear as it had a piece down the back and was tied round the waist with tapes. It had to be pressed in a certain manner, we were also issued with a lanyard and a square black silk which had to be folded into a loop, pressed, sewn up and when worn the lanyard was entwined with it.

There were dhobi sessions and in these we were shown how to wash and iron our clothes. As for the bellbottoms, they had to be pressed with seven horizontal creases to depict the seven seas.

I showed my first effort to the petty officer, who said, "Do them again."

"But I've got seven creases in them."

"Yes, but all the creases are below the knee. So do them again, properly."

The seven creases had to go most of the way up the bellbottoms and I also realised that the way everything was folded made it easier to fit in the locker.

I was measured for the number one uniform, which we had to wait for as it was tailor made. I polished my boots and shoes and they looked fine to me, but I got the impression they should've been spit and polished and you know what, to this day, I still don't know how to spit and polish boots and shoes.

One of the first meals I had was a pie and I said to the ginger bearded chef, "What's in the pie?"

"Prairie chicken."

What's that?"

"Rabbit," He replied.

It was very tasty. Once we'd settled in and got to know each other, we wrote letters and my mum replied by saying the first Sunday, she'd expected me back and had laid a place for me at Sunday dinner. I had the addresses of lots of girls and one day I came into the mess and the blokes shouted out, "Happy Birthday, Smiler!"

I was shocked as my birthday was in February. To my surprise I saw my bed was covered in letters. It was probably a novelty writing to a sailor, but it didn't last and one by one, most of the girls stopped writing.

We got down to the business of being trained as sailors. It was a week after we'd arrived when we had to see if we could swim. I'd been swimming since I was at junior school, albeit a mistake. It happened like this; we were walking around the swimming pool when I fell in. My form master noted that although I was struggling, I was managing to swim and so he coaxed me into swimming the length of the baths.

We also had to learn how to tie various knots, how to march, how to salute, how to stand to attention, how to stand at ease and rifle drill.

Which went something like this-Stood on parade as a class and assembled under the colonnade, P.O Brandon spoke to us.

"When I give the order of attention it's very easy, as all you do, is slide your left leg to your right leg. This is not the army and we don't bend the knee. This dates back to the days of sailing ships, when bending the knee to stand attention or at ease, took too long and the rating may lose his balance and fall over. So you lot should find it easy to do as we're on terra firma. This means, solid ground. So when I give the order Parade, attention, on the command Parade, you look sharp and wait for the next order."

He paused, "P-A-R-A-D-E, A-T-T-E-N-TION. Thumbs feeling for the seams of your trousers. Don't spread your fingers! Bend them at the first knuckle like this." He raised his arm to demonstrate. "Now you'll have to stop looking like a rabble, so I'll give the order, by the right dress. Greigson as you're on the right, you just stand to attention, and the rest of you will raise your right arm like so, with your hand bent at the first knuckle. The second rank will fall in behind the front rank and for distance; the right hand man will extend his arm forward to the shoulder of Greigson." He then bellowed out, "By the right, dress. Eyes front." And then added in a quieter tone of voice, "And what happened to you? Perhaps it's me, but as you'll notice you're the only man with his right arm still extended. Next time you pull yourself. Make sure it's together." P.O. Brandon was speaking to someone in the rank behind me.

"If you look out across the parade ground, you will see yellow spots. This is where you will fall in. First of all you will hear the command, *'Markers fall in,'* and during your training, Greigson, you will be the marker. You will, upon hearing the command, *'Markers fall in,'* double across the parade ground and fall in upon your yellow spot and stand to attention." (I would add here, every time I hear the word markers mentioned, it still reminds me of markers on the parade ground.) "Then the command, *'Parade fall in,'* will be given. You will all double across the parade ground; fall in alongside Greigson and dress. This is what I've just shown you. I'll now march you over to your spot and this will be your class spot whenever you fall in on the parade ground. One thing you never do, is walk across the parade ground, unless you're being marched across it. At all other times, you double across the parade ground.

P-A-R-A-D-E, right turn. Quick march."

We marched onto the parade ground and halted at our spot. Bryan had great difficulty with this, because his right leg and arm moved simultaneously. When we asked him about it he replied. "It's because of my last job, we were not allowed to walk around with our hands in our pockets, so I just let my arms hang by my sides."

P.O. Brandon then said, "Now we'll practice saluting, which is also very quick. All I want you to do, on my command of, 'To the front salute,' is pull your arm straight up to your head. None of this swinging it in an arc like soldiers; we raise the arm straight up the body to the forehead like this. And keep the palms of your hands facing your faces. This dates back to the reign of Queen Victoria, who was 'Not amused' by seeing the tarry hands of sailors."

So perhaps the college lecturer was right and Nelson was still in charge of the navy. But then I thought, wasn't he before Queen Victoria's reign?

We also learnt rifle drill and for this we used a 303, which apparently was the size of the bullet and the rifles were referred to as arms. We then learned how to slope arms, present arms, arms for inspection and there was an odd one called, arms at the short trail. It was used when on the march and instead of carrying the rifle at the slope, the rifle was carried with the arm extended, as if it were a bag or case.

Payday was once a fortnight and this involved queuing up, saluting with our right hand, whilst in the palm of our left hand; we held our ID cards and were paid in cash upon them. A GI, for saluting incorrectly, pulled me up. I was probably lucky to be paid.

One particular payday a GI called out across the parade ground. "Oi, you with your finger up your arse, and your brain in neutral! This is not a Sunday school outing. This is the Queen's Navy! Now double march, laddie."

At last our Number One uniforms arrived, which involved sewing on more badges, but this time they were gold, and we were finally allowed out. Or as the navy termed it, 'Ashore!' This struck me as odd, as we were already on the shore!

In fact our first trip was on Sunday lunchtime. I went with Ian and a few others to a pub. It was a modern concrete thing and had hot and spicy crisps on the bar, which were free. Naturally the more we ate these crisps the more we drank.

Apart from drill and being taught how to wash our clothes, with comments from P.O. Proudman like, "By the look of some of your sheets, I'm sure if they were left out in the sun, they'd hatch!" We also learned general seamanship, which involved learning various knots and lashes, and how to tell the left and right of a ship.

"The right hand side of a ship is called starboard and the left hand side of the ship is called port. This is because when a ship ties up alongside, it ties up on the left hand side, which we call in the navy?" The instructor asked.

The class mumbled a reply.

"I can't hear you?"

"Port sir!" The class replied loud and clear.

"Now of a night we have lights on the side of the ship to show other ships which way we're going. The starboard light is green and the port light is red. The easy way to remember this, is to use the phrase, there is no port left in the bottle."

One lecturer said we would have to go through a dummy war situation, which I was looking forward to. After all nobody was going to get hurt and it would be a bit of a laugh, but it never happened. In fact, the very day I was due to go on the rifle range, I was in the sickbay.

The previous night I'd been into Portsmouth, which usually entailed going into the NAAFI as the beer was cheap and upstairs they held dances. The only tune I can recall being played on the jukebox was *Sloop John B.* by the Beach Boys. We would then go onto a pub and maybe come back to the NAAFI for dances. On this particular occasion, I came back to HMS St Vincent drunk and as I went to lie on my bed in my No 1 uniform, I hit my head on the corner of my locker and said, "Oh no, not my head again!" (This was a reference to my crashing on my scooter when I wasn't wearing a helmet, which in those days wasn't compulsory.) There was blood pouring out of the back of my head. Greg cleaned my blood soaked collar, and I was taken to the sickbay, where I had some stitches sewn in.

I was released from sickbay the following morning and was told I was lucky not to be on a charge. This was because the person on guard duty would also have been put on a charge for failing to report me as drunk.

Whenever I was on parade, for either pay or going 'ashore', I was always told to get a haircut. When we got off the Gosport ferry directly ahead of us there was a barber's. I promptly went in and got a skinhead cut, well until it grew again. Then once again I'd get told to get a haircut. My hair is naturally curly and I really didn't fancy having it short on the sides and long on top.

Naturally I toyed with the idea of having a tattoo. As we had so many injections I thought of having a porthole tattooed on my upper arm, with the phrase, 'Open here for injections,' written around it.

There were two things I really enjoyed doing. The first was when P.O. Brandon raced P.O. Proudman's class in a large rowing boat, called a cutter. We'd rowed together before but this time it was a race and once we got into stroke, rowing as a team and skimming across the Solent in an open boat felt really good, and yes, my class won.

The second thing was climbing the mast. At one time H.M.S. St. Vincent had been a training ship (that's what the navy called it) for boys, hence the mast. It was like a mast on an old sailing ship and clambering up the rigging, I felt full of life, until reaching the top and stood on what is termed as the button. It was a bit scary, but brilliant. The button is like a stool but instead of sitting on it, you rest your bum against it and there's a certain way to wrap your legs round a bar and the ultimate thing to do is to raise your arms until they're level with your shoulders. Doing that and looking all around me over the walls and down upon Gosport was amazing. I believe it was to build confidence in boys, because in those days they could enlist straight from school.

At the foot of the mast I said to P.O. Brandon. "Back from the top, sir!"

"Carry on Saafend." This was both a reference to where I came from and my accent.

Finally, after six weeks basic training we were due to pass out and for this there was to be a final parade, but prior to that, the whole mess had their kit inspected. The officer of the day went round the room, inspecting our kit and asking each of us why we'd joined the navy.

He stopped in front of me and said, "Why did you join the navy?"

"To see the world sir." I replied whereas others had said to learn a trade. He looked at my kit and added. "In any other class, this layout would be good, but up against the standard of this class, it's poor."

It was the final parade and everything went well until we were marching along when the GI bellowed out, "To the left, salute!"

So I turned my head to the left and saluted with my left hand. What I should have done was turn my head to the left and salute with my right hand. Fortunately I passed out along with the rest.

P.O. Proudman had signed on and apparently, P.O. Brandon was due to leave the navy and as we were his last class, we all went for a farewell drink with him.

Having all passed our basic training, we went our separate ways. The Weapons Mechs. went to H.M.S. Excellent on Whale Island, which was The Gunnery School for the navy, I'm not sure where the Writers went to, but I think they went to Chatham and the rest of us went to H.M.S. Collingwood in Fareham, to study electronics.

CHAPTER THREE

Of the eighteen that had completed the initial training, we had been split into three groups to go to various training centres and so six of us turned up at HMS Collingwood. As Ian had been our leader at St. Vincent we nominated him to report us at the guardhouse and find out where our mess was.

Ian returned and said, "We have to go to E block, it's one of those over there."

I looked in amazement, as everything seemed so large. I swung my kitbag over my shoulder and joined the others in the long walk to our mess, which looked more like a four-story block of flats. "Ian I'm supposing those large blocks way over yonder, are to be our messes?"

"I suppose so." Ian replied.

"They look a lot better than the flats in Moss Side," Greg said, as this was a referral to where he came from in Manchester.

As we approached the parade ground I said, "How about walking over the parade ground? It'd be quicker than going round it."

This seemed to most of us a good idea but Ian dampened our spirits by saying. "I think we ought to walk around it."

We entered what was to be our mess for the next, (well I don't think any of us were sure how long we would be there for,) by a glass door and walked along a corridor. The walls were white and the floor was grey lino, off of which were the living areas. I looked into one and next to the window were two beds, that had on them blue and white naval counterpanes, at the top of the bed were folded some beige blankets, with a pillow on top. Next to the beds was a wooden wardrobe then two more beds and the wardrobes marked the entrance to the area. It smelled clean, with a hint of polish.

"Compared to St. Vincent, this place is so modern," Lenny said.

"Carry on, there should be a chief somewhere, who'll sort us out," Ian said.

I was amazed, not only by the newness of everything, but how many of us would be sharing a room, or should it be called a mess? I had no idea about this at all. Finally a bald leading hand appeared and addressed us; "You're the new influx of mech. apps are you?"

"Yes," we replied.

"Drop your kitbags, follow me and the chief will check you in and tell you the routine."

The chief, who still wore his cap, pushed it back on his head, exposing his dark receding hair, as he checked us in and said, "You will all be on the ground floor of this building and it is up to you, who you mess with. There will be four of you to a mess. So to start with, sort yourselves out into groups of four, get unpacked and changed into eights. That should take you until stand easy, after which, the leading hand will march you all over to the stores, to draw new cap tallies. Right, carry on."

Ian, Greg, Lenny and I shared a mess, leaving Bob and Johnny to fend for themselves. We chose a bed and locker and I said, "This is amazing! We've got a wooden wardrobe instead of a metal locker and lino on the floor instead of wooden floor boards."

"Same old beds though," Lenny said.

"And they have to be made up, as laid down, in standing orders." added Ian. "Still, that's easy enough to do, just put on the counterpane it looks as if the blankets are already boxed at the head of the bed, all that remains is to put a pillowcase on the pillow, place our sheets and pyjamas in the pile and Hey Presto! It's all done."

"I think I've got the hang of it by now, Ian." I replied. "But I thought as we're no longer in training, we wouldn't have to go through with this rigmarole of making beds in this stupid fashion."

"What did you expect, a hammock?" Greg asked. "Well no, but at least that would be easier."

"So perhaps you'd like your mum here to make the bed for you?" Greg asked.

"No, not that either. It just seems so stupid. I'll explain. Every night we have to strip down this pack and make our bed prior to going out, otherwise if we get drunk, then how the hell are we going to make the bed?" I replied.

"Smiler's got a point Greg." Lenny said.

"Thanks Lenny, so it would be nice to have the bed made up, without this blanket block at the head of the bed." I said.

"Why don't you three just get on with it, we'll try and work something out later on." Ian said.

"Maybe we can sort of keep the beds made, but still have this block at the top of the bed." I said.

"Go on then, and how do you propose to do that?" Ian asked.

"How about folding the blankets and sheets double and make them look as if the bed's stripped?" I said.

"You try it Smiler and we'll see how you get on," Lenny added.

I gave up with the bed idea, unpacked, made my bed, changed into eights and locked my wardrobe, undid the sliding window and climbed out of it saying, "Wow, get a load of this."

"Good job we're on the ground floor Smiler, otherwise I could see you getting pissed and falling out!" Greg added.

For stand easy (tea break), the leading hand appeared and said, "Go along to the NAAFI, it's just past the parade ground, you can't miss it and then report back here, to me."

As we walked along, I looked at some old huts behind the new blocks and said, "Look at those decrepit old buildings."

"They're probably the old messes," Ian replied.

Walking along I felt so relaxed, that I almost put my hands in my pockets. The NAAFI was huge, it had a jukebox, coffee bar and behind it were a bar and a dance floor.

"Blimey, this place is massive!" I said.

"Think about it Smiler, every electrician in the navy has to come here, at least once in his naval career." Ian replied.

When we were once again assembled in the mess the chief said, "Is there anyone under eighteen?" There was no reply, he continued by saying, "Is anyone twenty or over?" Again there was no reply and he added, "The reason I've asked is because if any rating is under eighteen, he can have a sweet ration and over twenty, he can draw his rum." He paused, looked at a clipboard and said, "As you are still in training, you will have to wear your uniform at all times and that, includes going on leave. Any questions?"

"When can we go on leave sir?" I asked.

"First of all, you have finished basic training and so I am referred to as chief. Next, about leave. Once you've finished work on a Friday, unless you are on duty for the weekend, then you may go on leave until Monday morning. Any questions?"

"What duties will we have to do?" Bob asked.

"As Mech. Apps. Your only duty is fire duty. This will consist of four of you sleeping in the hut, near to the parade ground and should there be a fire, then all four of you will rush along with the fire cart, to the fire. Most of the time, they are just fire drills. Also, two of you will have to go to the cinema. For that, you will have to draw lots. Any questions?" Nobody said a thing, "Right Bungy, assemble them outside and march them over to stores, to draw cap tallies."

As we marched along I mumbled to no one in particular. "Blimey, I could get lost here." "Keep quiet! This is the royal navy, not a Sunday school outing!" Bungy ordered.

Having been issued with new cap tallies, we were marched back to the mess where the chief addressed us. "Next, tie on your new cap tallies and when you've done so, report back here. And don't take all day!"

As we tied on our new cap tallies Lenny said, "It would appear that we are still in training, hence the bed layout."

"I suppose so." I dismally replied.

When we were once again assembled the chief said. "Whilst you're here, we expect you to do as well as possible in your exams, but apart from your electrical training, we like you to enjoy yourselves. So there are dances held in the NAAFI on a Thursday night and if you look on the notice board, you will see there are various activities for you to do, for example you can go gliding. But don't ask me; read the notice board, after all, as Mech. Apps, you should be reasonably intelligent. Any questions?"

"You mentioned about going on leave on Friday, if we're not on duty?" I asked. "This may seem daft, but I'm not sure how to get to London from here."

"Not as stupid as it sounds. Again, see the notice board for buses, or someone may even give you a lift to London. Otherwise it's back into Portsmouth and catch a train." The chief replied.

"What about washing?" Greg asked.

"Would that be yourself, or your clothes?"

"Both chief."

"On each floor of this building there are showers and heads, and as for washing clothes, there is a washing machine and a dryer." replied the chief. "Now your routine every day, except for the weekend is as follows. Get up, washed and dressed into eights, make your beds, have breakfast and then assemble on the parade ground and from there, you will be detailed off into groups to go to school."

"Where do we stand on the parade ground chief?" Ian asked.

"I'll get Bungy to show you." Replied the chief who looked at his watch and said, "It's almost time for lunch, so go and get your self something to eat and I'll see you back here in an hour." The chief then left the building, leaving Bungy to show us where the galley was.

The galley was huge, but the food was fine and once we'd finished we returned to the block. Bungy and the chief returned and we assembled by the stairs and the chief addressed us. "You will see on the table your mail. Should you wish to write to anyone, your address is as follows. E Block, HMS Collingwood, Fareham, Hampshire. If you should forget that, then it is on the notice board, which if you haven't already noticed, is behind you. Next, keeping your mess tidy. Bungy and I had a look around and I have to say that most of you have done well. I will mention no names, but suffice to say, that kitbags go in the wardrobe. Not under the bed! Also your weekend case is placed on top of the wardrobe, with your cap on top of it. Finally, your towel is to be placed on the towel rail that is on the front of the wardrobe. You are all adults and as such, I expect you to behave like adults. Next, cleaning duties. You will have to work out a cleaning rota between yourselves and the other members of the mess to clean the gangway, heads and showers. You will find cleaning materials in the cupboard under the stairs. You have finished basic training and so you should find this mess easy to keep clean. Any questions?"

The chief looked at as and then said, "As there are no further questions, I will leave Bungy in charge. Should there be any further questions, then Bungy will be glad to answer them for you. Today, you've had a rather easy day, but tomorrow, you will turn to on the parade ground, to start your education. Right, over to you Bungy." The chief said as he walked out of the block.

"As the chief said, you've had it easy today. The next you will hear is a broadcast saying secure. This means that the working day is over and it will be followed by rig of the day. You all seem fairly responsible, so I will leave you to tidy up your messes and correct the faults that the chief said. Any questions?"

No one said a word. "Good," Bungy replied, next listen to the tannoy and I shall see you all tomorrow." Bungy put on his cap and left the mess.

"What an easy start," Bob said.

"Right, let's see who hasn't stowed away their kitbags properly and also check your towels, case and caps." Ian said.

I picked my kitbag up from under the bed and placed it in the bottom of the locker. I set about writing a letter, which was interrupted by a voice on the tannoy saying, "Secure. Rig of the day, is half blues."

"How about after tea, we go and have a drink down the NAAFI?" Greg asked.

"Sounds good to me," Ian, Lenny and me replied.

"We'll ask Johnny and Bob and see if they want to come along as well?" Ian said.

That evening, having made our beds for sleeping in, all six of us went along to the NAAFI to have a drink. We wondered how the next day would be and how the others had got on at Whale Island, and hence we only had a couple of drinks as we all wanted to make a good start for the following day.

CHAPTER FOUR

The following day we followed the others onto the parade ground and then marched off to our classes.

The next week it was decided that all the Mech. Apps. were to be housed in the same block. We were then moved several floors up to an adjacent block. The Mech. Apps. were organised by a chief, who some said was a goody two shoes. Apparently his last ship had been the Royal Yacht Britannia. I later discovered that any rating on board the Royal Yacht had never, in their whole naval career, done anything wrong.

The chief was assisted by a three-badge killock (leading hand), who said, "I was on a submarine and we had an officer in charge who wanted us to change jobs. The only problem was, when we surfaced, we were in Weymouth."

At that time it meant nothing to me, apart from wondering why a submarine should be at the seaside. Later on I learned that the submarine should've surfaced at Portland.

Every morning we fell in on the parade ground and from there marched to our lessons to be taught about the navy and electronics. I noticed one of the ratings had a bent hat and as it appealed to me. I said to him, "How did your cap get like that?"

"I've been to sea and it became bent in my kitbag."

As we were still deemed to be under training, when we went on leave, we had to wear our uniforms. One evening we decided to go to Whale Island to see the others and they were amazed, as they could all wear civvies.

Of the lessons I can't remember much, just a few snippets, such as the Schooly (which is the navy's term for a schoolmaster, who was an officer), said, "Would you prefer to be either a control, or an ordnance electrician?"

Nobody knew what he meant and he said, "If you like to take things apart and discover what the fault is, then ordnance is for you. On the other hand, if you would rather have someone take it apart, then control is for you. Basically ordnance deals with large machinery and control deals with radios and the like. Furthermore, if you wish to be a control electrician, then you will have to do exceptionally well in your studies."

My brain pricked up at the word radio and I thought perhaps I would be able to be a DJ in the navy, but then not being very good at my studies, I thought I'd have to be an ordnance electrician.

"If you don't pass the exams, then you'll have to have a rescrub." The Schooly said, but rescrub had nothing to do with how clean we were, it was just a naval term for resitting the test.

During one lesson the Schooly drew some boats on the board; they depicted an actual battle in the First World War. The English Fleet was sailing along, when a German ship which was located about forty-five degrees and beneath the English Fleet, (well on the board it was). Just waited for each ship to get into a certain position and sink them.

So I asked. "Why didn't the fleet change direction?"

"They can't do that?"

"But they were getting blown up!"

Anyway, the whole situation seemed ludicrous to me.

Mixing with more blokes my whole world of music changed. Up until then I liked soul, plus the Small Faces, The Who and the Spencer

Davis Band. Upon hearing me mention the latter group, someone said. "Have you heard of Eric Clapton? He plays guitar like Stevie Winwood." (Who was the guitarist for the Spencer Davis Band.)

From Collingwood it was the first time I'd been home. I remember saying to dad as we drove along. "I really like the navy. I think I'll sign on."

"Now be serious son, you've only been in a short while. Think about what you're saying."

Once home on leave, I used to go along with my brother's friends to parties, one of whom was really into Eric Clapton and so at every party we went to, the album Fresh Cream would find its way onto the turntable. And yes, I loved that music.

Dave who was another Mech. App. but in a different class said to me, "Smiler how would you like to spend a weekend with me at my parents' home in Rickmansworth?"

I agreed and it was one of the most enjoyable weekends I ever had in the whole of my naval career. We were constantly bombarded with music. On Saturday morning we were in a coffee bar listening to the jukebox playing Semi-detached Suburban Mr Jones, by Manfred Mann. On Saturday night having returned from seeing a band, Dave and I sat in his living room, talking and playing Beatles Albums. We even went to a pub on Sunday that had a jazz band playing in the lunch break. That weekend went past so quickly and I said to Dave's mum, "I've really enjoyed myself but unfortunately, as I've spent all my money. I'm afraid I can't offer you any for your hospitality."

Dave's mother smiled, "As long as you've enjoyed yourself, that's all that counts. Plus it's nice to see some of Dave's friends in the navy."

One of the duties of a Mech. App was as a fireman. Four of us were chosen for the duty, and were billeted in a small shack but two had to go to the cinema. For the two left behind there wasn't much to do and for entertainment there was a record player. Although the only record I can recollect ever being played was Simon and Garfunkel's, Homeward

Bound. We were forever waiting for a fire call to the wrennery; at least I suppose that is what it was called, as it was where the W.R.N.S. (wrens) lived. I was actually on duty, when this momentous thing happened. All I can say was that the girls looked very nice, but as one wag said, "You wouldn't know what to do with it!"

One Saturday morning, having stayed at Collingwood I borrowed a bicycle which had the cable of the front brake wrapped round the handlebars, and in my ignorance I replaced the brake onto the front wheel, but there was no bolt to hold it in place. All went well until I braked hard. The front brake cable went round with the wheel and I went flying over the handlebars and cut my chin. I went off to sickbay where the medic put in a few stitches. At this rate, I could see my body being covered in scars from my misdemeanours. Fortunately I was still able to carry out my duties, and so I was not put on a charge for having a self inflicted wound.

On another weekend instead of going home I decided along with some others, to go gliding, it was one of a list of things that we could do. Finally it was my turn to go for a flight; I got in next to the instructor.

"Are you properly strapped in?" He asked as he looked at my harness. He then gave a signal to the Land Rover, which began to drive along and gradually we were hauled up into the sky and at a certain height, the instructor released the cable from the Land Rover. We hadn't risen very high when we started to descend.

"Sorry about that. The cable's broken; we'll give it another try." said the instructor.

We got aloft on the second attempt and it was just so peaceful. Nothing could be heard except the wind whistling along and below us, the ground just drifted by. I thoroughly enjoyed it but for the life of me, I don't know why I never had another go at gliding.

As Mech. Apps. we were very much into the Batman series on the television and when the episode ended with those immortal words, *'Can this be, Batman and Robin to die'* we tried to work out how Batman and Robin would get out of the fix they were in. I even sent off for membership to the batman club, but one week, the senior Mech. Apps. were flawed by the Batman Mystery, as Mr. Freeze placed Batman and Robin in a freezer. The way Batman and Robin got out of that fix was very technical. It was to do with a heater being used to freeze the ice and somehow or other, Batman used the heater to melt the ice. The senior Mech. Apps. were seething about this episode, because they had been unable to work it out.

For summer leave I worked with my brother and his friend Tom, digging out footings and doing general labouring work. Tom was a strong stocky bloke, who drank tea and coffee with his tongue hanging out. The money was handy, although I wasn't very good at labouring. I'd dug out one footing, compared to several of theirs. One day we got rained off and so we went to the cinema. My brother and I were stood waiting at Hockley station, when Tom appeared carrying an umbrella and my brother said, "Watch this." Tom then got the umbrella stuck between a lamppost and a tree; and we started laughing. Tom couldn't understand what we were laughing at.

One day in the builder's yard I lifted a block that was really heavy and said to Tom, "Try this and see what you think." As he was so strong I didn't think he'd notice.

Tom picked it up and said, "You're right Smiler that is heavy."

On another day we were digging outside some houses and I was singing. Tom and my brother overheard some children say, "Let's go up the other end and watch the drunk!"

So much for being happy in my work, but then, I had every reason to be. I'd met a girl, no not one of those that had written to me, most of them had long since stopped writing. Although I made love to this girl, it wasn't very good. More of a quick fumble on the sofa!

Over various weekends I did meet some of my old friends, two of whom had joined the army. One was in a band and said. "We have to wear these tight, maroon trousers, tighter than anything I've ever worn before."

I gathered apart from the trousers he liked the army, as opposed to the other bloke who said. "I was in Aden, walking down the road when I heard rifle fire. I carried on walking and thought I was sweating a lot. I put my hand up to my neck and there was blood. I was lucky to be alive. They gave me a medal for it. They can stick it and the army!"

It was in the autumn that part of our naval training led us into the New Forest, where we were split into several groups. Every day there was a competition to find items on a list. To do this we set off individually and I used to hitch around, chat to people and take in the scenery of the New Forest. We'd rendezvous of an evening, compare notes, camp out and cook the tinned food that had been issued to us. I thoroughly enjoyed this nomadic lifestyle. In fact the only problem about camping in the New Forest was the rainy weather. One night I lay awake in the tent and for some obscure reason we'd camped near a river. Had it rained hard we could have been washed away and with these thoughts running scarily through my mind, I felt a drip of water on my forehead, it felt warm and I felt that the Lord was looking after us and believed we'd be all right. I slept well that night.

The chief used to turn up and check on us and he said, "As it's raining so much, would you all like to return to Collingwood?"

Everyone was annoyed about this and we all said "No!"

Now ordinarily I am not a religious person, in fact when I was a baby my maternal grandmother took me away and had me baptised as a Roman Catholic. There it ended as I was never confirmed and if the truth were known, I actually joined the choir in a C of E church. Now this RC bit did me some good, because at Collingwood I met an attractive wren, who was also a Catholic and she enticed me into church. On the other hand, the Priest was not impressed with me, because I had not been confirmed and so he did not consider me to be a Catholic. The Catholic Chapel was only a small one and on Sunday it was not exactly bursting at the seams. I thought the clergy would be crying out for a congregation, obviously not. Needless to say, the romance with the wren was not one of those made in heaven.

It was a Thursday night and there was a dance at the NAAFI, an older Mech. App. said to me, "May I borrow that T-shirt?"

"Sure," I replied. I had the T-shirt as it looked like a sea jersey and thought I would be able to get away with wearing it, instead of the itchy sea jersey.

My other memory of the NAAFI was the jukebox and whenever it played The Small Faces, All or Nothing, and played the line *'Got to keep on trying,'* some wag would say, "Got to go to cleaning stations." It was a reference to the duties that electricians had to do but whenever I hear 'All or Nothing', by the Small Faces, I'm back in the NAAFI. Some of the Mech. Apps. thought I looked like one of the Small Faces, but I thought my brother looked more like one of them. Over the years I've been told I looked like one of the Searchers and Eric Burdon!

The older Mech. Apps. were nearing the end of their training, and were putting in for ships, some applied to go on submarines and not the nuclear subs, which were quite new then, but what were then called hunter killer subs. These were old submarines similar to those used in world war two. They'd applied for this type of sub; because serving on them they would earn more money. Rather them than me. A portly Mech. App. upon learning that he was now a killock said he'd sew the anchors everywhere, even on his underpants.

It was during my time at Collingwood I decided to learn to drive; I took lessons in a Singer Chamois and as we approached a dual carriageway my instructor said, "Put your foot down."

That car went pretty well, but I never did take my test there, the reason being I didn't do very well in the exams and neither did Lenny. We decided to change courses, Lenny left to become a Stoker and I went to Scotland to become an Aircraft Mechanic. It was only a week or so to Christmas and I wondered if I'd get Christmas leave? Also Greg left the navy, he said it wasn't for him and opted out.

CHAPTER FIVE

The train journey seemed to take forever and I arrived feeling rather bedraggled and hungry, put on my Burberry (mackintosh), over my No 1 uniform, and as it was the 16th December 1966, instead of a white front I was wearing a sea jersey, which although warm, was also very itchy. Stepping off the train, I hauled my kitbag onto my shoulder and walked out of the station at Arbroath in Scotland. Outside the station was a naval bus; wandering over to it I asked the driver, "Are you going to H.M.S. Condor?"

"Yes laddie, get on board."

"Do you think I'll be home for Christmas?"

"Aye, dinna fret about that. Ye'll be home for Christmas."

The bus ride didn't seem to take long as my thoughts were more about going home for Christmas. Approaching the gatehouse at HMS Condor the chief looked me up in a book and gave me a slip of paper saying, "You'll need this to draw overalls and rigging shoes from the stores. I've written down your mess, you'll find it easily enough."

"Yes chief," I replied and wandered along the road thinking I'd travelled back in time, because along the side of the road were Nissan huts. Eventually I found the one that was to be my mess, entered it and noticed the smell of floor polish. There were beds lined along the walls and the windows, were dotted along the mess at about head height. Having chosen a bed and placed my kit into a wooden wardrobe, I made my way to the stores.

Feeling somewhat isolated I wondered what the other members of my class would be like, but there were things to be done to take my mind off this. Firstly my cap ribbon had to be changed, then all the mech app badges had to be removed and sew on a badge that had an aeroplane on it, with the letters, AE underneath, plus my official number now began with an L, instead of a P. This was because having transferred to be an aircraft mechanic meant that I was no longer a general service sailor (fish head), but in the fleet air arm (airy fairy or waffoo). I had also been issued with overalls, canvas caps and aircraft rigging shoes.

The rigging shoes were excellent as they had leather uppers, moulded rubber soles and steel toecaps. The idea being that we would be able to walk on the specified area of the wing of an aircraft, to carry out maintenance. They were far more durable than the leather soled boots and shoes I had originally been issued with and we wore them all the time.

What struck me as odd, were that wrens were also being trained as aircraft mechanics. Why on earth they couldn't train as electricians was beyond me. But in those days wrens never went to sea and all the aircraft had land bases. Perhaps that's why the navy decided to recruit women aircraft mechanics.

Not only would I now have to learn my trade as an aircraft engineer but also had to attend classes to pass maths. This was something to do with promotion, for although I had 'O' level English Language and City and Guilds maths, the maths didn't count.

Once again there was a Schooly (officer) teaching us and he said to me. "You say that you have passed English Language, but from what I've seen so far, I would not have believed it."

This would mean carrying out another fruitless task, but by the time my course had finished, I had passed maths to the navy standards and as for English Language, I was exempt.

The civilian bus driver was right, as I did manage to get home for Christmas.

My parents and brother were staying with my Uncle Laurie and Auntie Cis in Chalk Farm and turning up at their flat wearing my uniform, my auntie said. "You remind me of your dad."

Dad was in the navy during the Second World War, although I think he spent most of his time attending courses, which was probably his way of avoiding going to sea. But he did end up on H.M.S. London, which was then a battleship and went on the Russian convoys and where none of the crew were allowed ashore. The pictures of him show the guns covered in ice so how on earth they ever expected to fire them, goodness only knows. As for Dad he was a wireless operator, which meant he did Morse code and had a winged badge on his arm. He told me how he was on a train and that two old ladies guessed that he was something to do with signals and when asked, Dad said he was.

"See I told you he was, I could tell by the pigeons on his arm," said one old lady to the other.

Having had a really great Christmas and looking forward to going back to Scotland. I was in Edinburgh, waiting for a train and entered the kilt shop and said to the assistant. "I wonder if you could tell me if I have a clan?"

"What's your name?"

"Bryson."

He looked it up in the book and said, "The name dates from Clydeshire in the 14th century and Perthshire in the 15th century."

"Great. What tartan can I wear then?"

"Well, your name doesna belong to any clan."

"Oh! Is there any tartan I can wear?"

He thumbed through the book and said, "You can wear this, it's the Stewart tartan."

"No thanks." I replied in my cockney accent.

"Och, maybe it's just as well."

On the first day of our instruction into the world of aeronautics a chief was stood in front of the class, he removed his cap revealing a full head of dark hair and said. "I will be your instructor for this the initial course in aircraft maintenance. My name is Chief Somers, so just call me chief. Over the coming weeks you will learn how an aircraft flies, how the engines work and for that purpose you will also be involved in practical work on aircraft engines. In the navy our prime concern is safety." He paused and said nothing, seeing if we had taken it in.

He carried on, "So let's say for example that an aircraft has landed, the pilot and navigator have left the cockpit, the first job will be to insert the pins in the ejector seat. Of course this will only involve fixed wing aircraft and not those that have propellers. But I'm probably jumping the gun a bit there, as you will be taught all about this. Another thing we are concerned about is corrosion. As almost all of our aircraft go to sea, then there is a serious problem with corrosion."

He paused and looked around the class and carried on, "I'll explain. As the aircraft are made of aluminium then whilst at sea, the salt water corrodes the metal. To compensate for this the aircraft have to be cleaned and covered in a solvent that keeps out the sea water." He stopped and had a worried look on his face, "I can see that some of you do not understand a thing I have said. Don't worry, all I am trying to do is give you an outline on the course that you will do and then, everything should become crystal clear."

Nobody said anything so he continued, "Right I shall draw a simple diagram that I would like you all to copy and I will label the parts. Incidentally the body of an aircraft is called a fuselage." He then drew a simple diagram on the board and said, "How does the pilot turn the aircraft to the left or right?"

During my training at H.M.S. Condor I learnt all about aircraft. How they fly, how they land, and so on, it was very fascinating. We also learnt about tool control. This meant that when we'd finished working on an aircraft, we were to replace the tool or tools in its compartment in the case. Hence when all work was finished on the aircraft, it could be ascertained at a glance if all the tools had been returned to their appropriate case. Meaning there would be no tools on the aircraft, when it took off.

We also learned about various methods to lock a nut or bolt in place. This either consisted of lock nuts and bolts, double nuts and wire locking the nut or bolt into place. Tea breaks, or as I had to get used to calling them, N.A.A.F.I. breaks, meant that we stopped work or our studies and a van appeared which was staffed by civilians and sold pies and tea or coffee.

The town of Arbroath was in actual fact just a small fishing village and their speciality was Arbroath Smokies, a term we also used for the local girls. An Arbroath Smokie is a haddock, which is then smoked and sold as an Arbroath Smokie.

Of a weekend I would usually go to Dundee, where I discovered the pubs opened at 5.00 pm, as opposed to English times of 6pm. Not only was the beer different, but so was the food. I found tasty little round meat pies, which were sold in most bakeries and called, bridies.

The beer served us was either light or heavy. Which to me seemed odd, as the light beer was dark and the heavy beer was light in colour. What the term light and heavy actually referred to was the strength of the brew. Hence a light beer was like an English mild and the heavy beer was a strong beer. I tried to be a man, drank the heavy and managed to get drunk and throw up.

There was also a good pub called the Bothy, where me and another bloke picked up two girls, who every now and again would say, "I dinna ken."

We never really got on as neither of the girls understood what I was saying and it was difficult to understand their accent. I later discovered *I dinna ken*, means I don't know.

Meanwhile back at Condor I'd decided to continue with my driving lessons but when it came to the test, I failed. Apparently that particular examiner had a reputation for being a bit tough, but I passed on my second attempt.

I'd also taken up judo, as did a wren and when it came to floor exercises, it's a good job there was nobody else around, because although we were doing exercises on the mat, I don't think what we were doing was judo.

Some of the other aircraft mechanics had formed a band, which performed in the N.A.A.F.I. bar. One song they did was 'Cut Across Shorty.' Which I'd learnt under duress when I was a scout. What happened was, we were camping in the Channel Isles, on Alderney and one of the older scouts told me to learn the words to the Eddie Cochran song, *'Cut Across Shorty'*, which I did. Now as for this band in the N.A.A.F.I., during the interval I approached the guitarist and said, "I can sing *Cut Across Shorty* better than your singer."

"OK then, in the second half we'll try you out."

So it was that I made my singing debut, but the offers of being a vocalist didn't come flying in. All that happened was that Ellis a mousy haired aircraft armourer, who played harmonica, (but I thought he only knew one tune) said, "Would you like to form a band?"

"I'll think about it, Ellis."

Having passed my driving test, the next thing was to buy a car. I was told about an artificer who was selling some. One had the wrong brake fluid in, but he assured me it would be all right. I made a few enquiries and was told that by putting in the wrong fluid would either swell the seals or shrink them. Either way, it sounded expensive. For the princely sum of £10, I bought a blue Hillman Husky and decided to take it home during the Easter break. Danny and Roy said they'd have a lift and share the cost of the petrol.

Driving home was a disaster. All three of us changed into civvies and Danny sat next to me and Roy sat in the back. During the night Danny said to me, "You've paid your road tax haven't you?"

"Yes."

"Well why don't you drive on the road?"

I was getting sleepy and kept veering off the road onto the kerb and to help me keep awake had my window open to which Roy said. "Can't you close the window?"

"Don't be silly. He'll fall asleep." Danny replied.

"When are you two coming back?" Roy asked.

"We've got rail passes." I replied.

Also the car started to go wrong. First of all something went wrong with the starter motor and Danny suggested removing it. This meant that when we stopped Danny and Roy had to bump start it, but later when we filled up with petrol I kept the engine running. We dropped off Roy and then just after London and prior to dropping Danny off. The exhaust either blew, or fell off. Having dropped off Danny, the drive down the Southend Arterial was very noisy.

My parents weren't too impressed when they heard this jalopy coming along and up their drive. Plus the whole street must've known I was home on leave. The car remained on the drive for all of my leave and presumably, my parents got rid of it.

During my leave, I went round to see Sue, she was about the only girl still writing to me. She was short, had long dark hair and wore spectacles. It was late when I left and as there were no buses, so I walked home. Ah, the folly of youth.

Meanwhile, back in the navy, in its wisdom the navy had decided that it would supply a bus and take us to Aviemore to go skiing. This was something I fancied having a go at, although I'd never skied before.

THE WRONG PATH

Once we'd disembarked from the bus we got our skis and went our own way. Novices like myself, were told to keep to the lower slopes.

I didn't feel cold but stared up at the snowy peaks of what to me looked like mountains. Sticking to the lower slopes, to my amazement I actually skied. Well, I'd never be an Olympic champion, but barring falling over a few times it went well. It was nearly time to return and I decided to ski down a gentle slope that was adjacent to a river. After all it wouldn't matter if I fell in, as I was already wet. I actually reached the bottom of the slope without once falling over. (Many years later, I had a go at water skiing. All I can say is, that it was the most expensive enema I've ever had!)

In a similar manner to Collingwood, the navy had decided that we should have a camping week in Scotland. This time I was unable to go because a bout of flu kept me in sickbay. During my stay, I read Sherpa Tensing's account of his climbing together with Sir Edmund Hilary to the summit of Mount Everest. Upon their return my classmates said that the chief, being our instructor also had his wife accompany the class on this expedition. Although they said the chief was like a mountain goat, it was apparently the wrong time of the month for his wife. She or he apparently dropped their luggage and tampons spilled out on the ground.

Finally it was time to take the exam that would qualify me as an aircraft mechanic. Upon hearing the results, I had come second. Not realising that the higher up one came in the class, the better chance one had of going to the Air Station of their choice. During the course I'd made up my mind not to work on fixed wing aircraft, as I didn't fancy working on any aircraft that had an ejector seat. The reason being, that once the pilot got out of the aircraft, safety pins had to be put in, this prevented the ejector seat accidentally being fired. Supposing somebody forgot to put in the safety pins one could inadvertently fire the ejector seat. (This was wrong, because safety was of paramount importance in the navy.)

The chief said, "As you've done well in your exams you are now a Specially Selected Aircraft Mechanic (S.S.A.M.). This means once you are qualified to maintain and qualified to serve (Q.M.Q.S) two different aircraft and passed all your qualifications for leading hand, you would then go back to school and if you once again do well in your studies, you would then be able to sit the exams to become a Petty Officer." This also applied to Steve a Scouser who'd come top of the class and he chose to go to R.N.A.S. (Royal Naval Air Station) Culdrose, H.M.S. Seahawk. What I thought peculiar was, why didn't the navy do this in the first place instead of trying to make me an electrician? After all, Artificers had a choice across the whole spectrum of trades in the navy.

R.N.A.S. Culdrose was the main place for helicopters and there was only one place available and this left me feeling very despondent, thinking it was the only place for helicopters. Fortunately, there was also one place available for R.N.A.S. Portland (H.M.S. Osprey), which also had helicopters.

H.M.S. Osprey was peculiar in that it was a centre for fish heads and airy-fairies. So it was that I was happy, but alone, as I travelled down to Portland, Dorset, where I would actually begin my trade as an aircraft mechanic.

CHAPTER SIX

On the 22nd May 1967 I wandered from the station at Weymouth and along to the seafront, where I looked out over the sand and watched the sun glistening on the sea. I felt ecstatic; as this was to be the first time I'd work on an aircraft. I found a bus stop where a man was stood smoking a cigarette and asked, "Excuse me, is this where I get the bus for Portland?"

"No it's along there; it'll go through the town, over a causeway, followed by gasometers. That'll be Portland."

"Thanks," I replied and walked along to the correct bus stop. As the bus left the town I looked over the causeway and the man was correct, in that once I passed the gasometers, I was in Portland. I walked up the slope to the base of HMS Osprey and seeing a sailor I said, "Excuse me, but I'm new here, where do I report to?"

He smiled and said, "Stand over there and take the bus up top. That's the living quarters and report there."

"Thanks, see you later." I replied and boarded the naval bus that turned left, past a couple of pubs and a cafe. On the left I caught sight of the RPO office and then it was into the naval dockyard until the bus went uphill to H.M.S. Osprey. Stood on guard was a large sign of an osprey, with a fish in its talons, I walked past it to a model of a torpedo that was in front of the gatehouse. Entered the gatehouse and the chief stopped reading a paper and stared at me. I said, "Naval air mechanic Bryson, reporting for duty."

He looked me up in a book and said. "Go past the wardroom, that's the first building you'll come across and then go into the next building and up to the first floor. You'll be attached to 829 Squadron. There should be a leading hand in the mess and he'll find you a bed."

Following the chief's directions I walked down a slope, and paused at the ancient building that was the wardroom to take in the panoramic view, of the Bay of Weymouth. Compared to HMS Collingwood and HMS Condor, Osprey was so small. I wondered if this was because most of the sailors were at sea. Reaching my mess and prior to entering, it occurred to me that it could easily have been as old as H.M.S. St Vincent. I entered the building and was faced by an ancient staircase that had a metal banister with a polished wooden hand rail. At the top of the stairs I opened the double doors and could smell wax polish that had been used on the dark wooden floorboards. I gawped in amazement, as this was the largest mess I'd ever seen. There were rows of beds on either side, plus the lockers were stacked up one on top of the other to separate the same amount of beds on the other side. I found the leading hand who had dark wiry hair, and a weather beaten face and I said, "I'm new here."

"No problem, I'm Jed, the mess killock. I'm supposing you are on 829 Squadron." He said in a West Country burr adding, "And you are?"

"Smiler, and yes, I am on 829 Squadron."

"Right Smiler, let's find you a bed and locker."

We walked along and stopped by a bed that had an empty locker by it and he said. "Put your kit in there and I'll show you where to put your kitbag."

Now I understood why during my six weeks basic training, my kit had to be folded in such a way. For this was the same type of small locker in which I had to stow all my kit. Plus, I could now officially wear civvies when I went 'ashore'.

I stowed my kit and changed into no 8's and rigging shoes and Jed said, "Don't forget your overalls."

I grabbed them, tucked them under my arm said. "Thanks". Jed said, "Report to the chief at 829 Squadron."

On my way to the heliport I thought H.M.S. Osprey was peculiar in that it was a centre for fish heads (general service) and airy-fairies (fleet air arm). Also being such a small place, there were no wrens stationed there. It would appear that long ago some wag named all the Air Stations after birds and the fleet air arm referred to them by place name, whereas the general service sailors referred to them by ship's name.

Arriving at the heliport I looked out over the small airfield, there were a few helicopters dotted about. I followed a sign to a long building, and entering the shack noticed a ginger haired chief stood behind a desk. I approached him and said, "I've been told to report to 829 squadron."

He stared at me and said. "You're not in training now, so as soon as you can, change your cap tally. In the meantime, go over to the wardroom and report to Lieutenant Nathan Smythe."

"Where's the wardroom?"

"Back up the slope turn right you'll soon find it."

I wandered past the hanger, entered a building and eventually found the wardroom, promptly knocked on the door and said as a tall slim officer opened the door, "I'd like to see Lieutenant Smythe."

Little did I know I was addressing the man himself who angrily replied, "Its Nathan-Smythe!" and then added, "You will now be working on a front line squadron and I hope you live up to my expectations of a specially selected aircraft mechanic. Now go back to the line shack and report to the chief. He'll tell you what to do."

How was I to know he had a double-barrelled name and you know what, from that day hence, we never really did hit it off.

I reported back to the chief who said, "Grab a broom and sweep up. If anyone wants help with anything, I'll tell them that you're a gash hand."

I swept up and found there was a room where people sat doing nothing but drinking tea or coffee. This was deemed to be a coffee boat that was run by two leading hands, Jimmy Rowan dark haired killock and Jake Fordham a blond killock. It was a rest room for ratings, for example, their helicopter may well have been flying. Jimmy and Jake probably made a small profit by selling coffee and other drinks to them.

But I hadn't done well in my training to end up as a sweeper. For lunch, it was back on the bus to the top and I was shown where I could get a new cap tally.

Gradually I learnt all about the Wasp helicopter, and one of my main tasks was to grease the rotor head in such a way that all the old grease was purged out. Naturally working with oil and grease made a right mess of my overalls. Jed came to the rescue and showed me how to wash them. He took me into the bathroom that had dark tiles on the floor and white tiles on the walls. Also on the walls were hand written signs that said, *'Hi Jean, Keep the bathroom clean!'* Jed said, "First of all soak them and lay them out on the tiles of the bathroom floor. Then pour soap powder over the overalls and scrub them. Then rinse off the soap."

Believe me it really did get them clean, although it was advisable to ensure nobody else was using the bathroom at the time. Then it was merely a case of squeezing away the soapy water down the drain.

For that first week I never went into Weymouth as I would have had to go in uniform, so I wandered around the mess and went down to the mess below mine and at the far end someone had pinned up the centrefold from Playboy magazine. The woman had dark hair and glasses, and her name was Fran Gerard, plus, she had the largest breasts I had ever seen. I wandered over to the poster and placed my hand under her breast and it filled it, and that, was only the picture. It put a whole new meaning on the song by John Fred & his Playboy Band, 'Judy in Disguise'. It was all about a girl that wore glasses!

At the other end of the mess there was a room with a few beds in it where someone had stuck up pictures of the Who. I was looking at them, when someone said, "Do you like the Who?"

I looked and saw that it was the sailor who'd told me which bus to get on when I first arrived. "Yes and thanks for putting me right about the bus earlier on."

"No probs. What's your name?"

"Smiler."

"Mine's Dan. I'll put on the Who if you like. Would you like a drink?"

"Yeh, love to hear the Who, I saw them a few years ago and they were amazing."

Dan put on an LP by the Who and asked, "What would you like to drink, tea, coffee or beer?"

We sat listening to the Who drinking beer from a can. I discovered that Dan worked on the Wessex helicopters of 737 squadron.

There were three types of helicopter at Portland. Wasps, which were small and carried four or five crew. They had four doors and their role was to be attached to a frigate. This is the helicopter which I was to work on and the chaps who'd been to sea with Wasps said, "It's brilliant and even the fish heads weren't all that bad."

I was on a front line squadron and as far as I knew, I had a very good chance of going to sea on a frigate, as opposed to an aircraft carrier.

Then there were Wessex Mk 1 helicopters of 737 squadron. This was a second line squadron whose role was to train people and as a consequence the squadron never went to sea. Finally, there were a couple of Whirlwinds that were painted in dayglow red and blue. These were old helicopters that still had piston engines and were used as Search and Rescue (S.A.R.) helicopters, as opposed to the Wessex and Wasps, which had gas turbine engines. The navy in its infinite wisdom seemed to put old helicopters on Search and Rescue.

Both the Whirlwinds and Wessex were stored in another larger hangar, at the other end of the heliport, which also incorporated a line shack.

Portland is a natural harbour and at various times, the following ships docked there; submarines (these were the small hunter killer types, which had a diesel engine), MTB's (which apparently went so fast that seamen could not stay on them for long, as the vibrations could cause varicose veins.) From up high in Osprey these small, but fast boats could be seen heading out to sea, leaving in their wake a long, white V formation of froth.

During the long summer nights as we were returning to the mess, somebody said, "You see that view?"

"Yes." I replied.

"Well you probably think you're looking at ships on the sea. Actually, there are men underneath who just move the props around. You look next time we come out; they'll have moved the ships around."

Most of the time at the squadron I was sweeping up and so to keep myself amused, I had a small portable radio wedged in between my shoulder and neck.

One hot summer's day I was outside the line shack when Jimmy Rowan appeared and shouted inside, "Here, come and look at this!"

Jake Fordham joined him and Jimmy pointed at me and said, "Now look at that. He's just won the ugliest bloke of the year competition." They laughed and went back inside.

One thing about being in a mess with so many other blokes meant there was always somebody who you'd get on. As a consequence I used to go 'ashore' with Den, Ian, Richie and others whose names I cannot remember.

A lot of the time at the heliport there was nothing to do, so I used to sit outside the line shack and put flowers, or rather daisies in my hair. Well, it was the time of hippies. But it was on one of these ponderous moments I realised what the three-badge killock had been on about in Collingwood, when he said that his submarine had surfaced in Weymouth. Of course, they should have been in Portland.

During my early days at Portland, Taffy Thomas, a gangly aircraft mechanic approached me and said. "Can you do me a favour?"

"Yeh sure. What do you want me to do?"

"I need someone to marshal in my helicopter." "I'm sorry, but I've never done that before." "But it's easy."

"Maybe for you, but as I've never done it, I don't know what signals to give."

"You're useless." He replied and walked off.

The heliport had large circular markings on the ground where each helicopter would take-off and land. They then flew into a set of parallel lines, which I suppose, served as a type of runway. I made it my duty to find out what signals I had to do, for both landing and take-off. As Taffy had said, there really wasn't much to marshalling, but for that first time, especially when I'd never done it before, it was a bit nerve racking. There were signals to give to start the engine, engage rotors and then what to do for landing and take-off.

Then I made a horrendous mistake. During the day, pilots would be trained to fly by instruments; to give them a foretaste of night flying. This entailed fixing amber screens inside the windows of the helicopter and the pilot would then wear a dark visor, which gave the appearance of night and he had to fly only by instruments. I put in the amber screens all right but when the pilot in charge landed, he said, "Did you put those screens in?"

"Yes."

"You haven't cleaned them or the windows. So next time, do it properly!"

Well, I thought, *why bother; after all, they were supposed to be flying by instruments.*

One day the line chief said to me, "I hear that group of yours, The Beatles, has had their latest LP compared to a classical composer."

"Oh you mean, *Sgt. Peppers*. Yeh, it's not a bad LP I think they're on about the track called, *She's leaving home*. It's something to do with the way there is one tune laid upon another."

"Yes probably. Now get along and sweep out the crew room." Portland was excellent for one thing and that was weekends. At three o'clock on a Friday afternoon, work stopped and the majority of people went away on leave. When I went home for a weekend, I usually went with my brother to see a band.

There wasn't much to do in Portland and not much more to do in Weymouth. In fact I managed to find a pub, which had three people in it, and one of those was the barman. Of a weekend in Weymouth, well during the summer, there were groups on at the pavilion. Failing that, there was a disco in the town. It was a bit difficult to find, and not only did they play records but also had a band and one of the numbers they did was *Soul Finger*. That guy in the band really did blow a mean trumpet. It was an odd time musically, there was still great soul music being released by Motown, Stax and Atlantic, but then rock bands like Cream were emerging.

At other times I would go along with some others, to pubs that had folk singers appearing. Mind you, when you've heard one gravelly voiced singer perform, *"Ole Stewball was a Racehorse."* You've heard them all, but they were good fun and after a few pints, everyone joined in with the singing. There was one good thing about Weymouth and that was the beef burger stall. It was near to the bus depot and made excellent burgers. Whilst waiting for a bus after a few beers it was just the thing to eat.

Talking of waiting for a bus, there's one guy who made us all laugh. He was with his girlfriend at the bus stop, when she got chatted up and taken from him. The odd thing being she was chatted up by a girl, not a guy! This kept us amused for weeks.

I decided to get mobile and bought an Austin Sixteen, which was a monster of a car. Unfortunately something went wrong with it and so two of us decided to strip down the engine. And, it never did get put back together.

CHAPTER SEVEN

Part of the duties of an aircraft mechanic, or in fact any rating working at the heliport, was to guard the heliport of a night. This meant working two-hour shifts throughout the night. There were several of us and we all had to sleep overnight down at the heliport. In the summer if you were lucky you could go to bed and get up in the morning without having to do any duty. This was due to the helicopters performing night flying duties.

I was once teamed with Carlos to 'guard' the heliport and we headed out to the far end of the airfield near to the gasometers, as we entered a boiler house. I said, "What are these gasometers for?"

"Smiler, think about it, they hold fuel for ships and aircraft."

Inside the boiler house Carlos and I sat down and chatted to the night watchman, it helped to pass the time on what was otherwise, a rather boring duty. Also, on Portland there was a prison for adults and youths. If there was a breakout, then the guard was doubled and we had to wear helmets. Luckily whenever I was on duty, nobody broke out.

Once whilst on guard duty we had to go and watch a helicopter being pulled out of the sea. It was a Wessex and as the crane lowered it down, the water dripped from it and sadly, the pilot was still sat in his seat. This was the first time I'd ever seen a dead man, but being quite a distance from him, it made no impact on me.

On a lighter note, I went to stay with Den for a weekend at Stevenage and on Saturday night we went to a large dancehall. Whenever the band changed, they played Time is Tight and the band was replaced on a turntable by another band. Den and I met two girls who said they would be going to Weymouth for their holidays. The one I was with was the more attractive and I asked her,

"Have you heard that LP by the *Moody Blues, Days of Future Passed?*"

"Yes, it's pretty good." She replied.

We said we'd see the girls in Weymouth, but I'm sure they didn't believe us. Well sure enough when they turned up in Weymouth, I spotted them and said I'd meet them later on. When I did go back into Weymouth, Den wouldn't come with me. I think this was because, just for once, I had the more attractive looking girl. So I took with me Richie, who was a good laugh, but like me, not the best looking bloke in the world. Well, I never did see those girls again. I thought Den was not really playing the game, after all, when I'd been a mod I used to go chatting up girls with a mate of mine, called Dave. We took it in turns to have the more attractive girl in the pair. In the end we knew it would work out fine.

Later in the year, Den and I met two Swedish girls who came from a place called Vaxjo. They made such an impression on us, that we said we'd visit them next year in Sweden. All we got was our passports.

It was November when I finally became Qualified to Maintain and Qualified to Serve (Q.M.Q.S.) Wasps. As a consequence I was now promoted from a Naval Air Mechanic (N.A.M.) 2nd class, to N.A.M. 1st class. This meant sewing on new badges, as I now had a star above the aeroplane and I got a pay rise.

Having reached the dizzy heights of a N.A.M. 1, I decided to go on a course, to help me gain promotion to Leading Hand. For this I had to take exams in my own trade, fire fighting, safety equipment and damage control.

Fire fighting concerned what action to take if an aircraft caught fire, safety equipment was all about life jackets, dinghies and general safety and damage control was about the action to be taken if a ship was in trouble. Then there was a separate subject, 'Power of Command'. This involved being in charge of a squad of men, who were known colloquially as, 'awkward squad'.

The fire fighting course was most peculiar, for not only were we lectured about fire fighting, but we also had demonstrations of what to beware of, if the fire fighting suits were not impregnated with some anti-fire fluid. For this demonstration, two aircraft handlers (chock heads) were dressed in fire fighting suits and then the chief, set light to both suits. One burnt away, whilst the other didn't burn at all. I later got to know both of the chock heads, and asked one of them, "Why did you do it?"

He replied. "It's something to do and breaks the monotony." "But, aren't you afraid of getting burnt?"

"No." He laughed. "We both wear another suit underneath. Anyway, we're trained to fight fires and work with flames lapping around us."

As for the damage control course, it was above my head. It would have been easy if I'd been to sea and could relate to the things we were lectured about. Stuff like soft wedges, hard wedges, soft bungs, hard bungs, which were to be put in the ship's side if water was gushing in. This all meant nothing to me.

Whilst on the course, things for me took a dive. A group of us had just left the greasy spoon, (a cafe near to the heliport, which we often frequented), and feeling relaxed I had my hands in my pockets.

"Oi you, with your hands in your pockets. Over here!"

"Shit!" I'd forgotten there were two regulating offices, one up top and this one in the dockyard. I entered the office.

"Id card." The leading regulator said.

I looked in my pockets. "I've left it in my locker."

"Cap!" I handed my cap and he said, "Name and rank!"

"Naval air mechanic Bryson."

"But that isn't the name in this cap."

"I can explain. My cap was bent and this leading hand has just been promoted to petty officer so, I took his cap." as this was written down, I tried not to laugh.

The leading regulator said to the regulating petty officer (RPO), "I'll do him for silent contempt."

"No, you can't do that." Replied the RPO, "put him on captain's defaulters."

Now the problem with my caps was that I was always bending them, to simulate being at sea. Every time I went on parade, I was told to buy a new one. So naturally when I found one in my size, in good nick, I took it.

The PO who owned the cap saw me and said, "Come 'ere you!"

I wandered over and he said, "You had a nerve, taking my cap. In future, ask first! I do not like to be called by the regulating office about something I have no idea about. Do you understand?"

"Yes."

"I've said that you asked me, but I am not happy about this situation." He then walked off.

The next day I was up in front of the Captain on defaulters. I pleaded guilty and was sentenced to ten days number 9's.

This meant no shore leave, stoppage of pay and two hours extra duties a day, plus, something I was really not looking forward to, laying my kit out for inspection every day. Luckily I did not have to do the last bit. As for the extra duties it meant getting up earlier, mustering in front of the Duty P.O., who then assigned us some work. Having blotted my copybook I thought, *if ever the Royal Yacht has a helicopter on board, then this is one rating that would not be going on it.* It was at this stage that I walked along the lower path, to the NAAFI bar. It was small, rather depleted, but very cheap. I bought a scrumpy top, and even though it was only 9d (about 3p in today's money) it is not something that I can recommend, but my punishment soon passed.

Whilst undergoing punishment I informed Terry, a blond aircrew man, who from what he'd said previously, had often undergone no 9's.

"This is the first time I've had to undergo punishment Terry."

"You're having me on."

"No, I'm not, honest."

"You do surprise me. How are you coping?"

"All right. But tell me, when you underwent punishment, how did you cope with the stoppage of shore leave? After all, from what you said, you were at sea at the time."

Terry smiled and said, "I only underwent punishment when we were at sea. In port I was all right, well until the last few days of leave."

"Thanks Terry."

When I took the Power of Command exam I thought it was easy, as there was a rating wearing gloves. Straight away standing in front of them I bellowed out. "You with the gloves on. Remove them!"

"But it's cold."

"Did I say you could speak? Have a look around and I think you'll find that you're the only one wearing gloves. Now get them off!"

After that it was easy and I had an 80% pass mark. As for the rest, I failed abysmally and was duly informed when I would be able to take the exams again.

Later on I got to know the rating who wore the gloves and he said, "I used to work on Buccaneers. I'd spent a long time polishing the windscreen of my aircraft and we thought it was late in coming back, but then we heard it had crashed. I went along with the others to look for debris and I found the pilot's helmet. I picked it up and found that his head was still in it. I threw up."

I was also chosen as one of the ratings that would assemble in Weymouth by the war memorial, for the Sunday Remembrance Parade.

I had visions of not keeping quiet when the minute's silence was on. *After all*, I thought, *had Remembrance Sunday ever stopped any more wars?* It was not to be, so like a good sailor, I arrived in Weymouth, marched to the war memorial and did my bit.

Then the big day arrived. 16th February 1968. I was twenty and so, was able to draw my first tot. I was first in, but this was a mistake, as I then had a magic tot glass in that it never emptied. As a result I was sick and thrown into cells. Boy was I miffed. Being a Friday I was going home to see John Mayall's Band. I was allowed home on the Saturday and that night went to see Duster Bennett and Peter Green's Fleetwood Mac at the Cricketers pub in Southend. It was brilliant, although my parents were not very pleased about me not arriving home on Friday.

CHAPTER EIGHT

On Monday I was paraded before the Captain. I told him that I would give up my tot and he replied. "Highly commendable. But you will be unable to do that, until the new moon. As you've shown remorse, I sentence you to ten days number nines."

This was my second stint of No 9's and it was like water off a duck's back. In fact I got up early as usual and one day the Duty P.O. said, "OK carry on. No work for you lot today."

So I went back to bed. This was fine until the Duty P.O. arrived at my bed and to say he was not very pleased. Would be making light of it.

I was once again taking the course to help me become a Leading Hand. During one lunch break I had to clean the torpedo which was situated outside the gatehouse. As such I turned up late for the lecture on Safety Equipment that was being given by a Leading Hand I'd got to know, called Ray.

I bounced into the room and said, "Sorry I'm late Ray, I've been cleaning the torpedo."

"I know. The others told me Smiler, sit down."

Ray then asked a question and I put my hand up and answered it, to which Ray replied, "If Smiler knows, you should all know it."

Eventually the tests came round and they were mainly verbal. I went into the one on damage control and the Chief said. "The ship has a hole in the side and there's water gushing in. What do you do?"

"Put a wedge in the wall."

"Would that be a hard, or a soft wedge, and what do you call a wall on a ship?"

I thought for a moment and then said, "Soft wedge, and the wall of a ship is called, a bulwark."

"Right, you've got a man with a broken leg below decks and you have to take him to sickbay, which is several decks up and forward. How do you do it?"

"Best you put him in a stretcher."

"Any type of stretcher?"

"Yes."

"How would you solve the problem of lifting him between decks? Bearing in mind, he has a broken leg."

"Ah, best you tie him in then."

"Ever heard of a Robinson stretcher?"

"No." After all, for me Robinson only made jam, or is it barley water?

I then answered a few more questions and left. It was a similar case when the bearded chief who ran the fire fighting section confronted me.

"What would you find in a foam extinguisher?" He asked.

"Foam."

"Right, you have an aircraft that's landed and it's caught on fire. What would you do?"

"Get the fire tender and get it to squirt foam over the aircraft."

He then went on to ask me more about this and I just waffled on about more fire tenders arriving and squirting foam. In fact I think the aircrew would've drowned in foam. Having done all the exams we had to line up and enter one at a time to hear our results. The officer looked at me and said. "Name and rank."

"Naval Air Mechanic, Bryson."

Upon hearing my name, the officer looked at me in a loathsome way and angrily said, "If it can be done, you've done it! You've actually done worse this time in fire fighting and damage control, but you've done better in your own subject and safety equipment. If it were up to me, you'd have failed. As it is, your overall mark is a pass. Now get out!"

For those that are interested, the side of a ship is a bulkhead and a Robinson stretcher is one that is specifically designed to carry injured personnel about a ship. It actually has bits that can be folded over the patient to ensure he stays strapped in. As for the foam extinguisher, I really don't know what chemicals make up the foam, which is presumably what the chief wanted to know.

As for Ray, the safety equipment killock, I'd known him for quite a while. If I had a spare moment I would walk around and have a chat to some of the other guys. Ray had dark hair, with a bald spot at the back and one-day I entered into the safety equipment shack and one of the guys said.

"Look at this Ray!"

It was one of those occasions when I'd got fed up with being told to get my haircut and so I'd had it cut really short. When Ray turned up, the same guy said. "Ray won't get his hair cut that short. In case it doesn't grow again."

"I find I'm attracting the older woman with this bald spot." Ray replied.

"Ah, but do you have much choice?" said another safety equipment rating.

I left them having a go at each other, but I must admit the safety equipment section had served me well, because I had an old holdall (grip), which had a broken zip and so they took it out and replaced it with Velcro strip. This was superb.

Having passed my tests for a leading hand, I decided to further my education and take math's GCE. I'd discovered there was a schooly that taught such things, plus, I had visions of being a pilot. Once again, I was allowed one afternoon a week to go and study. All was going well until one day I approached the chief and asked. "OK if I go off and do my studies?"

"Sorry, but you're needed to work on the helicopters."

After that, it was difficult to get away and so I gave up studying for any more GCE's.

Then the guys in the squadron voted me to be the squadron representative. To which the line chief said. "Why'd you pick him? He's very mouthy."

"That's it exactly. He'll go and do what we ask." The leading hand replied.

The main gripe was the food. Now, I could not challenge the cooks on their culinary skills, but there were rumours that the stores officer had a Bentley and the chief cook had a Mercedes. I got up early in the morning, went down to the galley, told the cooks who I was and said. "How come you don't use fresh milk?"

The cook just shrugged his shoulders and I reported this back to the squadron who then said, "Next time you have a meeting, ask for a food committee. They've got one at Lee. (This was a reference to Lee-on Solent, the headquarters of the Fleet Air Arm).

At the next meeting I asked for a food committee and was told it would be considered. I waited until the next meeting and at the end; I once again raised the issue of a food committee. To which came the reply. "Commander S (stores) won't hear of it."

I reported back to the squadron and then gave up being their rep. At one time there were some students who wanted to look around and so the line chief grabbed me and said. "Take this lot round and explain to them about the helicopter."

I wandered off to the hangar with the students in tow, walked around a Wasp and explained what it did and one chap looked up to the flat things above the doors and said. "What are they?"

"That's the flotation gear. If the helicopter should go into the sea, these things expand and keep the helicopter afloat."

"Aren't there any guns on it?" Another chap asked.

"Actually, we can fix torpedoes beneath the helicopter, or else we can attach missiles, but if we do the latter, there has to be an aircrewman flying with the pilot. This is because pilots have been mesmerised into following the missile, and crashing."

Suitably impressed, the youths left.

CHAPTER NINE

Shortly after I'd passed my exams to qualify in airmanship as a leading rating, I was transferred to 737 Squadron. I was not amused, as ever since I'd joined 829 Squadron I'd been applying for a small ship's flight. Upon arriving at 737 Squadron, it was the end of all my hopes of going on board a small ship, because as far as I knew, Wessex helicopters were only on board aircraft carriers.

As a distraction I volunteered for different things one of which was awkward squad. This meant being part of that squad that was similar to the body of men I'd drilled to gain power of command as a leading hand. Having been drilled around a few times, the officer in charge called me out and spoke quietly saying, "For the next person, whatever he tells you to do, do it wrong."

"Ok." I replied and returned to the ranks.

Yes, I did everything wrong that could possibly be thought of, but the chock head in charge never noticed a thing. Then he gave the order, "To the left salute!"

This I did with my left hand and not once did the person correct me on what I'd done and after the officer had finished examining the chock head, he called me out and said. "Now show the squad how to salute with the left hand."

I started off well saying, "Saluting with the left hand, is similar to saluting with the right hand, except that it's done with the left hand."

The only thing was as I demonstrated to the squad; I was in fits of laughter to which the officer said. "I think you should take charge of yourself, before you try to take charge of the squad. Now go back to the ranks."

The line shack of 737 squadron was incorporated inside the hangar and in the crew room amongst the card playing fraternity could be heard somebody slamming down their fist which, as it had rings on it, rang out around the room. This I later discovered was Tony Danvers playing cribbage, as whenever he slammed his hand on the table, he called out his points.

One sunny day as there wasn't much to do, Ian Price and I went for a walk around Portland, it was something we'd do to get away from naval life. We stopped and sat down on the grass and I said, "I don't want to work on Wessex. I wanted to stay on 829 and go on a frigate. So I thought perhaps, I could fail to become Q.M.Q.S. on Wessex."

Ian said, "Smiler, you can't fight it. OK, so you don't want to work on Wessex, but you know what they'll do?"

I shook my head.

"One of the chiefs will one day come out to you, point at a helicopter and say, *What's that?* And you'll say, *a helicopter.* Hence from that day on, you'll be Q.M.Q.S. Wessex. I know, I've seen it done."

"Yeh, I suppose you're right."

In the tale cone of a Wessex helicopter was a large flotation bag. Therefore if a helicopter was laid up for a while and not being worked upon, it was possible to just lie on the flotation bag and have a crafty snooze, actually it was a shame there weren't any wrens around.

Working on 737 Squadron entailed turning to, at different times, whereas the rest of H.M.S. Osprey appeared to work a 9-5 shift. 737 Squadron also did night flying, and as such, on some days, I had to turn to at lunchtime and work through until late at night. It was while

I was on one of these late shifts that I ignored the early morning call and stayed in bed.

The Duty P.O. caught me and said, "Get up now! This is no place for idle loafers!" On the other side of the mess he repeated what he'd said as he found another rating still in bed. He looked at both of us and said, "You two are on defaulters".

The Officer of the day said, "Why were you in still in bed, at this time of the day?"

"I don't have to turn to until one o'clock and so, I thought I'd stay in bed."

"I see. If that's all you've got to say for yourself. I sentence you to one day's fourteen's."

The other rating was sentenced to the same punishment, which was two hours extra duty. We carried out our punishment and completed it by the time we turned to. As we did the extra duty we both cursed the fish heads.

Another friend said "I'm going to become a diver. This involves undergoing various tests and then, if I want, I can take the navigation test and become an S.A.R diver."

"Wow that sounds good and they don't do anything except sit in the crew room all day, waiting to be called out."

"Plus, I'll get more money for being a diver and more money for being aircrew."

"Even better, good luck."

In the mess, I got chatting to Paddy Murphy and said, "I've not seen you in the heliport, so what do you do?"

"I work on PTA's; they're pilot less target aircraft." "What's that?"

"They're like large model aircraft and we travel around the world and the gunners on ships use them as target practice. The only thing is, they sometimes hit them."

"Isn't that what they're supposed to do?"

"No. They're only supposed to have near misses otherwise it costs a fortune to repair them."

"So how do you get to these different locations?"

"Fly, of course. We have to live out of a suitcase."

"Wow! Sounds like my kind of a job. So whereabouts are you situated?"

"In the dockyard. Call in sometime."

"Thanks Paddy, I'll do that."

Having managed to find where the PTAs were housed I entered the shack and looked at these small red aircraft.

I've already mentioned commander S and the Chief cook had very nice cars, well there were two other flashy cars at Portland. One was an E-Type Jag, which was owned by a pilot, word had it he came from a wealthy background and the other flashy car was a Mercedes Sports. This belonged to a rating who'd inherited some money. Word had it that if a rating showed up the captain of the ship, he would be told to leave the navy. As far as I know this never happened, I never met the rating but he was pointed out to me and was very smartly dressed. He wanted to leave the navy, but I never found out if he ever achieved his goal.

At Easter I boarded the ferry, along with, Wilf, Ian Price and another rating also called Ian, to St. Brelades in Jersey. The weather was pretty good, but we only stayed a week, although we did have a go at surfing, which I don't think any of us were good at. Mind you, we didn't exactly have the waves for it.

For the second week of my leave I went to my parents, who had moved from Hawkwell to Bridge Lane in Golders Green. I arrived at night and had no idea of where they lived. I phoned up my Auntie Cis, "Hello Philip, how are you?" She asked.

"Fine thanks, but I'm not sure where mum and dad now live. Do you have their phone number?"

"No, they've only just moved there."

"I'm near to the Brent Bridge Hotel, they can't be far away."

"Good luck and let us know how you get on?"

"Will do and I'll get mum or dad to give you a ring."

When I did find where they lived, I thought the flat was very nice and they used to sit in the kitchen, mainly because in the summer, they could open the door and overlook a park, it gave the flat a feeling of being in the country. In winter there was a fire that kept the kitchen warm, heated up the water and a radiator in the hall.

CHAPTER TEN

I returned to Osprey to find that things were changing for the better. As Osprey only had a small amount of accommodation, volunteers were asked to live out in Weymouth and the navy paid for it. Those that went on the first wave had a brilliant time as they moved into flats and pooled their resources so that at the end of the month they could have a party. Naturally when they asked for more people to live out of Osprey, Den and I were among the volunteers.

The only problem was instead of us having money and finding our own accommodation the navy found it for us.

OK, so I did manage to share a room with Den and the food was put on the table at certain times but it was all so regimental. I can only assume that they used to run a boarding house for holidaymakers and as such, saw this as a means to a regular income. Being away from Osprey I'd taken to wearing the lining from my Burberry, over a shirt and jeans. This was a throwback to my days as a mod, when on hot days instead of wearing my parka; I would just wear the lining.

Unfortunately the landlord didn't like the way I dressed and informed the navy, who had me moved back to Osprey.

There were rumours' going round that a driver was required to work over the summer leave. This meant working whilst everybody else went on leave, and then going on what was termed as retard leave. I'd been told that it was a doddle. I volunteered and had to take a test drive with a civvy in the short wheel based Landrover.

I turned up at the appropriate place in the dockyard and the civvy said. "Get in the Landrover and I'll give you directions."

I started the Landrover and we drove off up the hill and up to the lighthouse, putting the Landrover through its paces and when we got back to the dockyard the civvy said. "You're too fast for me laddie."

"Does this mean I've failed?"

"Yes."

I thought this was rather odd, as every Landrover driver I'd seen, drove like a lunatic. Having failed the driving test, I asked if I could go on normal leave, this was also declined. I ended up on gate duty at the heliport. Actually, this was a right doddle. I just had to stand at the gate wearing half blues, white belt and gaiters and every other night I would have to patrol the airfield. It was on one of these occasions that I'd got out of bed in the morning, dressed in my 8's, went up to Osprey had breakfast and changed into half blues, belt and gaiters.

I relieved my opposite number on the gate and an officer was stood there who said. "You're late. This chap's been on duty all night."

"So have I."

The officer then apologised and wandered off. One day I was stood there, trying not to fall asleep, when an officer approached me and I promptly saluted him. He returned my salute and said.

"No need to salute me. I'm a customs man."

I believe 737 Squadron was also used to train pilots, which was why we had to turn to, for night flying duties. Plus, I discovered much to my amazement that a few of us were about to go to sea, presumably so we could get the hang of life on board a ship. It also enabled pilots to get the feel of landing and taking off from a ship.

My first trip to sea was on board R.F.A. Engadine, which was a merchant ship used by the Royal Navy. R.F.A. stands for Royal Fleet

Auxiliary and these ships could be anything from tankers to cargo vessels, which allowed the Royal Navy vessels to refuel at sea (RAS). On the rear of the Engadine was a landing platform and a hangar that housed two helicopters.

On boarding the ship, one bloke was seasick and we hadn't even left the harbour. As for me, I said to one of the older ratings, "They've got a woman on board."

To which he replied, "No. You've just seen Angie."

"Yeah, that's right. A woman."

"No. It's a bloke."

"But he's got tits! Alright, they're small ones, but he has got them."

"Yes, that's Angie all right."

"Are you sure that it's a bloke? What with the tits and the high voice?"

"Yes, that's Angie all right."

Angie was indeed a bloke, albeit a gay one and his job on board the ship appeared to be that of a cook. Nevertheless, it took me a while to suss out that he was in fact a bloke.

On the Engadine we did a spot of vertrapping. This entailed loading and unloading goods to the helicopter. The pilot had to fly off with the load suspended beneath the helicopter. The object was to try and get the load to swing as little as possible; because once this started it was difficult to stop, which also made the helicopter difficult to fly.

We were out on the Bay of Biscay, which is renowned for its rough sea but when I was on it, it was as calm as a millpond. In fact I was off duty, sunbathing, eating a choc-ice, reading Alfie and oddly enough, I later went below, to watch the film of Alfie. Yes, it was certainly a hard life at sea.

It was during my stay at Osprey they had Navy Days, which meant the public could have a look over a naval vessel and so I thought I'd have a look over a submarine. I queued up and when I got to the front the PO said, "You didn't have to queue."

"Oh it's all right; I just thought I'd have a look over a sub."

I went down inside the submarine and even though the hatches were open, it was smelly and ever so small. It was like living in a tube, there seemed to be nothing in it but a gangway with a few beds stowed on the side. I took my time but was glad to surface and leave the submarine; I could not believe how anyone would volunteer to serve on one. Rather them than me.

But then things changed, as I was going to be drafted to Culdrose in Cornwall and from there, to a ship. I had since learnt that County Class Destroyers had a Wessex helicopter on board them. I had an idea that by going to Culdrose to work on a on a front line squadron, would mean going to sea on an aircraft carrier.

Now some of you may recall when I first qualified as an aircraft mechanic, I wanted to go to Culdrose, but that seemed so long ago and I'd become acclimatised to the easy life at Portland.

CHAPTER ELEVEN

On the 15th July 1968 I arrived at Helston in Cornwall and caught the bus to H.M.S. Seahawk (R.N.A.S. Culdrose). Having reported to the gatehouse and told where my mess was, I walked across the vast parade ground and stopped at the mast, glanced across to the N.A.A.F.I. when someone came up to me and said, "Are you all right?"

"I was just trying to take in the size of this place and I'm on my way to my mess."

He pointed and said "All the messes are over there."

Arriving at my living quarters, which were single storey buildings joined by a long corridor, I entered and said, "I'm new here, any chance of a bed?"

"Yes," said a leading hand, "There's a pit over there and use the locker next to it."

The locker was once again a wardrobe and I began to unpack saying, "This place is huge, so where's the heads?"

He got off his pit, took me to the corridor and said, "Down there is where you'll find the bathroom and heads."

"Thanks." I replied.

At the other end of the mess was another door that opened out to a grassy area, which in summer was used for sunbathing.

I once again met up with Ellis and also became friendly with Gary, Tony, and Stan. Our main link was with music. I recall one day going into Helston and Gary, a blond haired chap said to me.

"Will you get me a Bob Dylan LP? There's a track on it called, *It takes a lot to laugh, it takes a train to cry*."

But that's jumping the gun. For my first night at Culdrose I had a few drinks at the N.A.A.F.I. bar and bumped into a chap whom I'd met in Portland and he said, "Hi Smiler. Want to buy a car?"

"No thanks."

"It's a Citroen and I only want forty pounds for it. Perhaps you could buy it together with some of your mates."

For a fiver, I had an eighth share in a Citroen, which I used mainly to transport me to and from work. I should explain here, that Culdrose is a huge Air Station and at one time had Gannets, so naturally it had a landing strip, but when I arrived there it just had loads of helicopter squadrons. Turning to in the morning meant waiting in line for a bus to take me to the other side of the airfield where my squadron was housed.

One day as many of us as possible crammed into the Citroen, I never drove it. Instead we had a chock head drive us. This was a mistake; he drove like a lunatic and lowered the suspension. After which, the car never seemed the same.

The others knew when I'd arrived because I used to enter the crew room singing, *I'm so Glad*. It was a song that Cream performed on their first LP, Fresh Cream and much to the annoyance of one of my fellow room mates, I would rise every morning, wander over to the galley, have a bowl full of Coco Pops and a cup of tea. I would add here, the food at Culdrose was so much better than at Portland, every lunchtime there was a steak grill, with a choice of either having a beefsteak or a gammon steak. So it crossed my mind, were the rumours about the Chief and the Commander at Portland, being on the fiddle true?

After breakfast I returned to the mess, and would put on the Fresh Cream LP, sometimes I would act as if I had a guitar and one rating said. "You don't hold a guitar like that. It's a lot wider than that."

Obviously they weren't in tune with bands like Cream and Jimi Hendrix, who were all electric and so played slimmer guitars. One of the aircrew looked at the cover of Fresh Cream and seeing Jack Bruce (bass and vocals) dressed in a flying jacket, leather flying helmet and goggles, plus Ginger Baker (drums) dressed in some sort of military jacket and Eric Clapton (guitar) wearing goggles, the aircrew man said. "It's a disgrace. They've made a mockery of flying gear."

What did I care? They made brilliant music, but my first big shock came on Friday at Culdrose. It was gone three o'clock in the afternoon and I said to somebody. "Don't we finish now?"

"What!"

"Well when I was at Portland, we finished at three and went on weekend leave."

"Oh no, you work until five here."

Also I'd managed to procure a small picture of Alfred E. Newman (of Mad Magazine) and inserted it in my ID card instead of my picture. It was all right until a policeman stopped me and when I showed him my ID card, he was not impressed. A few days later he happened to stop the Citroen that I had a share in and when he asked who owned the car, they rattled off amongst other names my name. To which the policeman replied. "Shouldn't he be with you?"

Quite frankly, I'd given up with the car.

On a Saturday morning I used to visit Helston and do my washing. This did not impress the lady in attendance who would throw us out, because washing our overalls in her machines ruined them. On one occasion I used a friend of mine's Hillman convertible to get to Helston. The rear window was plastic and made it difficult to see anything out of it, I only used it the once. The chap who'd lent me the car was a rather tall and gangly bloke called Mickey and he went up in my estimation, as he'd been in the Fleet Air Arm Field Gun Crew.

At that time during the Royal Tournament at Earls Court, there was a race every day between different sections of the Royal Navy.

The sections were Portsmouth, Fleet Air Arm and Devonport. It was quite an honour to be chosen to represent your section and all Field Gun Crew members had a jacket of a different colour to depict whom they were running for. The Fleet Air Arm was green, Devonport Red and Portsmouth blue. There were also rumours about men losing their fingers, as they'd dropped the pin that went into the gun. I never thought to look at Mickey's fingers. In fact when I was stationed at Portland we actually went up to London to watch the field gun crew and the announcer said we were in the audience. It was a brilliant night out. Sadly with government cut backs or whatever, the Field Gun Crews no longer exist. They were certainly an excellent display of fitness and teamwork. Hence I was in awe of Mickey.

Of a night I used to pop over to the N.A.A.F.I. and have a few beers and one night a chap entered a box, which was positioned just inside the hall, on the far side by the dance floor. This chap then played a few records and said. "Now for a track, from the late, great, Otis Redding."

Wow! I thought, that's what I fancy doing, being a DJ. I did make a few enquiries, but never actually got round to becoming a DJ.

There was also a pub in Helston that brewed its own beer and on special occasions, like Christmas and Floral Day, the landlord made a special brew. I entered with Gary, who went to the loo, and I said to the barman. "Two special brews please."

"But there's only one of you."

"My mate's in the toilet."

"I'll pour out one for now and when your friend arrives I'll pour out the other. This is a strong beer."

On that count he was right, but even his normal brew was quite strong. I popped in one Saturday with Stan, we were doing our usual thing of going to Falmouth, but thought we'd have a pint before catching the bus and believe me, when Stan and me boarded the bus even after one pint we knew we'd had a drink. But then we probably hadn't eaten.

Once in Falmouth we'd frequent a pub that had a superb jukebox, have a few beers and buy a pie. One of the records I recall being played was the flip side of a Canned Heat record and the tune was "World in a Jug". Sometimes in the afternoon when the pubs were closed we would go to the pictures and always knew when Ellis was there, even though we never saw him, as he was into sniffing Dab It Off. It smelled awful so how Ellis could saturate his hanky with it and inhale the stuff was beyond Stan and me. After that Ellis was in a jovial mood and we would once again go to the pubs where Ellis would somehow manage to get us invited to parties.

This all ended when Stan and I went to sea. Prior to going to sea, I was on leave and went to a pop concert at Woburn Abbey, where my brother and I camped out for the weekend. Amongst the performers and bands we saw were, Jimi Hendrix, who headlined the bill on Saturday, Tim Rose, Donovan, Tyrannosaurus Rex, (it was probably their first live appearance. There were just two of them on stage, Marc Bolan and Steve Peregrine Took.) and Taste, who were the hit on Saturday and headlining the bill on Sunday was John Mayall, but the best band on Sunday was a band called Family.

Then I returned to the navy and had to face up to being on board H.M.S Eagle, the second largest aircraft carrier in the navy. I don't know about Stan, but being with 820 squadron on board H.M.S. Eagle, was my worst nightmare. We were to be billeted in 6W0 mess. Now I'd better explain the numbering system. The numeral at the front meant how far down below the top deck you were, but being an aircraft carrier, this was half way up the ship. The ship was then sectioned off from front to back, or if you prefer, from the bows to the stern. A, would be at the front of the ship and Z right at the back, or stern. So it was that I found myself living below the waterline in the stern of the ship.

CHAPTER TWELVE

To get to the mess I had to go along several decks, and down through numerous hatchways. The lockers were the same size as the first locker I'd ever used, at H.M.S St. Vincent, which now seemed like eons ago. I was allocated a bunk, which was the top bunk in a three-tier system. This was a bonus, as it never had to be made, I'll explain.

The bedding, which consisted of a mattress cover, sheets and blankets, was all zipped inside a plastic cover. Turning to meant hinging the bed, unlike the two bunk beds below me, which during daylight hours were used as a seat. The bottom bunk was the seat and the middle bunk was the back to the seat. There were about eighteen of us in the mess. Luckily, we were not all there at any one time.

One of the guys was into surfing hence he was stationed at Culdrose, but whenever he was off duty he would be off to Newquay to surf. Being at sea was a bonus for him, as he went along to the divers and managed to obtain the material to enable him to make his own wet suit. He even made a hat and boots.

He said. "This will allow me to surf throughout the year."

At that time the ship was about to embark on manoeuvres with other navies from NATO and so we spent six weeks at sea, in the Arctic Ocean. Plus, I was not going to be working on the helicopters, instead I was to be misemployed on between decks party. Stan was also misemployed, but he was a P.O's mess man.

One day he'd drawn their rum ration, about a gallon and so I said to him. "Stan, how about I have a tot?" "But Smiler, they'll miss it."

"No they won't, we'll top it up with water, they'll never know."

Stan was reluctant but nevertheless, I did manage to draw out a tot and boy was it good. You see unlike the tot I drew; this was neat and undiluted with water. Well it was before I added the water to make up the level. I offered Stan a sip but he declined.

As for myself, I was to be Captain of the Heads. Mind you, they were not just any old heads, but they were officers' heads. In fact I had two lots to do and one, was the personal head of the Captain. Now just in case you wondered what a head is, it is the naval term for a toilet.

I wrote home and when mum heard she wrote back saying, "You're supposed to be specially selected, not some shithouse cleaner. I don't care if it is the officers; it still amounts to the same thing."

My messmates had a right old laugh about this. Actually, being Captain of the Heads was a bit of a doddle apart that is, from when we had rounds and on this account one week I had the best heads and the following week the worst. When I had the best heads, it was the Captain's, but when I had the worst, I think the officers had some do, as the toilets were full of spew. This was only a daytime job and so of a night I went off to the galley, which was used as a cinema and also sold ice cream.

Being in the Arctic Ocean on exercise meant of a night there were no lights on the weather decks, while the other decks had red lights. A weather deck is as the name implies, open to the elements. I found a route to the galley from my mess using a minimum of weather decks, but then some fish head said. "What you do is use the light from your lifejacket and you'll be able to see along the weather decks."

This was a brilliant idea and meant no more tripping over bits on the weather decks.

For lunch, I would draw my tot and then go to the salad bar and the food was delicious. We had beans, radishes, corn, lettuce, tomatoes, plus sausages, ham, various cheeses and ice cream. Marvellous.

I turned to late one afternoon and the bosun said, "Fell asleep did we? OK, never mind."

He then detailed me off to do something. One day I had a leak in my heads and had to report it and it went something like this. "I've come to report a leak in the heads."

"Where are they?"

"They're the officers' heads on the starboard side, no wait. They're on the port side."

"Look, that's the front of the ship and that's the back. Are they on the left, or the right?"

I pointed them in the correct direction.

Then I got a huge surprise. It transpired there was a certain day for me to have my laundry done. So I tied up a bundle of my dirty washing and went along to the middle of the ship, where a Chinaman confronted me.

"I'm new."

"OK, this your number."

This was brilliant, plus they also sold underwear. They were fancy coloured boxer shorts made out of cotton. I was told the Chinese had a stream running through their quarters, and they bashed the clothes with stones and then just sat around playing Mah Jong. However they did a brilliant job of cleaning my clothes but there were always notices either in the ship's paper or posted about the ship saying, the Chinese had worked overtime on the button-smashing machine. Once again this was a reference to the buttons being smashed on our number 8's, or whatever.

During my break I wandered up to the flight deck and further up to the goons deck and watched the hive of activity going on below, on the flight deck. There were chock heads towing aircraft with tractors, they either towed them to the side or onto the catapult, where two chock heads secured the strap. The Flight Deck Captain then signalled the aircraft for takeoff, and so it was catapulted off the deck and rose up into the sky. The aircraft on the carrier at the time were, Sea Vixens, Buccaneers, and Gannets, plus of course Mk 1 Wessex Helicopters. Meanwhile, at the rear of the carrier, aircraft were landing. They had to hook on to a selection of arrester wires. I later discovered that our pilots were also landing on United States Carriers and they came back saying, "It's like landing on an airfield."

As it was so small, I don't think the Yanks managed to land on the Eagle. Mind you, as I looked out across the sea I could see the other ships in the convoy, it was as if we were at war but then I suppose we were, well we were playing at it. In between the ships were icebergs and alongside the Eagle was a magnificent silver helicopter. This was the Yanks S.A.R. helicopter and was later used in the Royal Navy and called a Sea King and believe me, it certainly lived up to its name.

Being the second largest aircraft carrier in the navy the Eagle only had one lift; unlike its sister ship Ark Royal, which had two lifts. The lift was used to move the aircraft from the hangar to the flight deck below and whenever it was in operation, bells rang out across the deck to warn anyone in the vicinity, that the lift was in operation.

Plus, it goes without saying; the water in the heads was icy cold. One fish head remarked.

"This is the longest that I've been to sea for. Six weeks without putting in to a port."

While another fish head got drunk and threw himself overboard. Rumour had it he'd been drinking aftershave. Now why he couldn't drink beer I don't know. What I've omitted to tell you is, that when you draw your tot you're also entitled to a few cans of beer. Even then ratings were saying. "If they ever stop issuing the grog, then there'll be more drunks on board ships."

What they were referring to was that when a man drew his tot it was one man, one tot, but with the cans of beer if a man didn't want his beer then someone else could and would, have it.

Of an evening if we were not on duty we had to change out of working clothes into rig of the day, which was usually half blues. Sometimes, we had an officer inspect our mess.

I said to my mess mates, "Any chance I could have a go at being a DJ?"

"Phone him up," was the reply.

The next night, I did a programme. I wandered up to the radio station knocked on the door, and when it was opened I introduced myself the guy said. "Pick out some songs from the collection and off you go."

I don't know how long a programme I did, whether it was half an hour or an hour, but I really enjoyed it. One song that I do remember saying, "Now here's one you can sing along to," it was The Court of King Caratacus by Rolf Harris. The following day I asked the others what they thought.

"So that was you was it? Sounded all right to me."

Whilst at sea, we were still paid once a fortnight and had to muster in the hangar at a certain time, to collect our wages. I was on my way to getting paid when I bumped into Ray, the safety equipment killock from Portland. As we left the gangway and entered the hangar my shoes clicked as we walked.

"Smiler, what are you wearing?"

"Shoes. Why?"

"Have you got metal tips on them?"

"Yes. I had the heels done."

"You do realise that you could be done for wearing them?"

"Why? After all I'm not working on aircraft; I'm only the shithouse cleaner."

"That's not the point. You could cause a spark, which would ignite the fuel from the aircraft."

Luckily, I never did get done for wearing the wrong shoes.

So it was that my second time at sea ended and it was back to Culdrose, where I was in for a shock.

CHAPTER THIRTEEN

I left H.M.S. Eagle and 820 squadron thinking that I'd completed my length of time on servicing two types of helicopter. Now I'd be able to devote my time to becoming a leading hand. Oh boy was I wrong! It appeared the navy had other ideas for me.

I was once again stationed at R.N.A.S. Culdrose (H.M.S. Seahawk). Much to my horror I discovered I was to be drafted to H.M.S. Eagle again. This time I was to be part of the S.A.R. (Search and Rescue).

820 Squadron was to be disbanded, due to the updating of the Wessex Mk1 helicopter to Mk 3 helicopters.

Now for some technical info; the Wessex Mk 3 helicopter was equipped with a radome, which could be dropped into the sea enabling it to seek out submarines. For the non-technical minded a radome is a large blob, which is lowered into the sea and emits radar bleeps, this enables the radio operator perched up in the helicopter to find submarines.

As opposed to being mis-employed I was now part of a small team led by a pilot, Lieutenant David Stanton working on a helicopter.

What's more, I was also billeted with the other members of the S.A.R. apart from those who were living ashore.

This may sound odd to you as I was already based on land. But ashore meant married men could live at home in Helston or wherever, with their families.

To take up the rest of the vacant beds in the mess another small ship's flight were billeted with us, but they were off an R.F.A. One of them used to drink the poor man's black velvet, which consisted of scrumpy and Guinness. One day he said to all of us, "I was in a pub drinking this awesome concoction when one of the local's said to me."

"If he don't eat, after drinking he. Then he, eats he."

"The local was saying, that as scrumpy gets its sour taste by hanging meat in it and gradually the cider eats away the meat, then so it would be, that the scrumpy would eat away my stomach."

One of the R.F.A. team was huge and had a black beard. He said to me. "Do you like the Rolling Stones?"

"Yes." I replied.

"Would you like to buy this for six bob?"

It was a copy of their latest album, 'Beggars Banquet'.

I rummaged through the change in my pocket and replied, "I've only got five bob."

"That'll do. It'll buy me a few beers."

So from that day, instead of Cream, I played the Rolling Stones.

Meanwhile back at work, I was in the office of Lieutenant Stanton, the dark haired officer commanding the S.A.R. He perused my documents, looked up at me and said, "Well, it looks like you've finally got your small ship's flight."

I said nothing. After all, the Eagle was hardly a small ship, but having said that as part of a team, I got on well with the other members of the S.A.R. and all the officers apart from Lt Stanton, were referred to by their first names.

At Culdrose I was once again back into my old ways of Saturday's spent in Falmouth with Ellis and Stan. I was still heavily into music and you may be wondering what on earth I was moaning about, well I'll explain. With the S.A.R. we all went between Culdrose and the Eagle, it was one of the times that I'd not long returned from leave. Having finished work at Culdrose I was sat on the bus en route to my mess. When the PO aircrew diver said to me. "Your hair needs cutting."

To which I replied, "I could get a job anywhere with this length of hair."

He replied, "You have a job though."

Yes, I thought, but I'd rather not have it. Things came to a head and I got so fed up with being told to get my hair cut that I shaved my head and this met with very mixed comments. The chaps in the navy said, "You'll get done for that."

Now this I could not comprehend but was duly informed that if the ship went down they would not be able to drag me out by my hair. Again this seemed odd to me as first of all I was on land and also, what about baldy men, how would they get dragged out of the sea. Mind you, John Glass, whom I'd nicknamed Hinge Head, you see he was bald but had a flap of hair combed over his baldpate, which flapped about in the wind and looked like a hinge.

That night there was a dance in the NAAFI and so Pete, a stocky aircraft mechanic, lent me a slaughter man's cap and I also donned a pair of dark glasses I'd bought in London. They looked very much like aircrew sunglasses and I thought I looked the business.

At that time, next to the hut where we worked was the photographic section and so one of the photographer's said, "May I take your picture?"

"Sure," I replied.

He wrote on a board, 'Baldy,' and said, "Can you hold this?" It was a bit of a laugh.

He was a Londoner and really enjoyed taking pictures, he showed me some he'd taken as a hobby and I got the opinion that once he left the navy, he would still be taking pictures.

Whereas in Falmouth some hippy said to me about my baldness, "Far out man, shows you don't give a damn!" Now that, really did reflect my opinions.

Whilst at Culdrose our flight was visited by an admiral and the flight chiefs did not want me to meet him, but he asked to see everyone. We were all duly lined up in the office and the admiral went along asking us questions, mainly about if we were married.

He got to me and said, "What about you, are you married?" "No sir, and I ain't even half married."

As he was leaving he thanked the chiefs and said, if he had to choose, he would be happy to have me on his team.

It all changed when I was once again billeted on board H.M.S. Eagle, only this time I was in 6W2 mess. There were fifteen of us and I had the bottom bunk. The top bunk was perceived to be the best, as it was very rarely made and became the prized possession of the horizontal kings. These were the chaps who when not on duty, spent their time in bed. I never found having the bottom bunk to be a problem because whenever I turned to, I merely had to zip it up. We also had living in our mess a storeman and a chef. The latter received the brunt of our displeasure, but eventually he did put on a good spread for us.

What this now meant was that my time was split between Cornwall and Plymouth, where the Eagle was docked. I remember going ashore at Plymouth with the others from the S.A.R. and I was trying to speak posh. Usually my accent is cockney, or as it's now termed estuary. So there I was in a pub and I said, "What do you think of my posh accent?"

To which came the reply. "Actually, you sound gay."

So ended my days of trying to speak posh. I later went into the local dance hall, but the bouncer said as he looked at my cord jeans, "It's not your scene." He was right as I didn't stay long and as I walked out he remarked, "I told you so."

As for my time on board the Eagle, it was a dramatic change from my life as Captain of the Heads. Every time the aircraft were flying, the

S.A.R. had to be in the air. The Eagle set sail and as it did the various aircraft Squadrons flew on board. We now had on board the Mk 3 Wessex, as I've already mentioned, Sea Vixens, Buccaneers and Gannets, which as far as I can remember were the last aircraft to have propellers, or in this case, two, which counter rotated.

Rumour had it, that one of the gannet pilots made several attempts to land on the flight deck, but as he couldn't manage it, he was told to return to the land base.

My day would start by someone turning on my bed light and as it shined into my face in the morning, telling me to turn to. I washed, dressed and went up on the flight deck and waited until the helicopter arrived. I watched mesmerised as the sun rose from the sea and spread its orange glow all around. I stood and looked in awe and said. "Wow! The sun's rising."

"Another J.D." Came the reply.

A bell clanging rang out across the flight deck. This meant the hangar lift was in action and gradually the helicopter appeared on deck and was towed towards us.

I then had to assist in spreading the rotor blades of the helicopter. This entailed either Pete, or myself sitting on top of the rotor head, the others jiggled the blade up and down whilst Pete or I, banged home the pin. This done, we would go below and have breakfast. After which I would return to the flight deck watch the helicopter take off and return to the Burma Row.

This was a small passageway, which ran inside the large tower on the right hand (starboard) side of an aircraft carrier. I would sit there with my back against the chimneystack reading paperbacks and drinking coffee, which the leading chockhead would make and sell to me. Whenever the helicopter landed, I would run across the flight deck with the logbook, refuel it, climb up the side of the helicopter and get the pilot to sign for a rotors running refuel. The blades were spinning just a foot or two above my head, and then it was back to the Burma Row.

At mid-day I would be relieved by Davey Jones, (a large aircraft mechanic) draw my tot and get something to eat followed by bed. I would then turn to at six in the evening, until flying finished. This was followed by maintenance on the helicopter, a night flying supper and bed.

The following day I would draw my tot, have something to eat and start work at mid-day and finish at six.

One night I was sat in the Burma Row reading, when Ed James, a short electrical leading hand approached me and said. "There you are. We've been looking all over for you."

"Why? Has it landed?"

"Landed! We've put it away and it's down in the hangar!"

1968 rolled into 1969 and somewhere along the way, the Queen who was on board the Royal Yacht, reviewed the fleet. That night the Queen, God Bless Her, ordered splicers. Otherwise known as splice the mainbrace, which meant we were given an additional tot that was issued in the night. I was stood alongside Jock Stewart (an aicrewman), drinking my rum when he poured some of his ration into my glass. Why he did that I don't know, but I did get rather tipsy.

I went below; slid open the door of our office stumbled inside and said to Paddy Ryan and John Glass, the two chiefs in charge of maintenance.

"Back from splicers."

"Get below Smiler. We've finished for tonight. And by the look of you, so are you." They replied.

It was about this time, I went into the adjoining mess, which housed the helicopter squadron and together with Dan, (whom I'd first met in Portland) took some records down into a storage place below. I was getting into the stuff we were playing, when someone, threw some cold tea over us. We promptly left and I returned to my mess, where I was asked who did it?

Jock Stewart was ready to punch the guy's head in, until he discovered who'd done it and then realised that the bloke's wife, was friendly with his girlfriend. As for me I just shrugged it off. It was just another idiot, who thought he was being big. Naturally I had a shower and as for my clothes, the Chinese laundry would be able to clean them.

At the time we also had an electrician called Sparky and he gave me a really weird book to read entitled, 'The Naked Lunch,' by William Burroughs. It was all about drug addicts, presumably as I was into rock music it was also assumed I was into drugs, which I wasn't.

As we were often between the Eagle and Culdrose we kept most of our kit on the ship and one day we just threw everything on board the helicopters and flew from Culdrose in Cornwall to the Eagle. As we flew over Plymouth, Glenn, the flying stoker opened the door of the helicopter and said, "There you are, Plymouth from the air."

Glenn had started life in the navy as a stoker but he'd done the various tests for aircrew and diving and became the flying stoker. He said to me once, "Have you ever been diving Smiler?"

"No," I replied.

"You should try it some time, on the surface you may have all sorts of problems but once you go down under the waves all your problems disappear. It's a completely different world."

"Yeh, I think I'll try that some time."

The aircrew then changed and also, the storeman in our mess left and was replaced by Terry, of whom the last storeman said. "You'll never get on with Terry."

How wrong he was. I got on really well with Terry.

CHAPTER FOURTEEN

One weekend when I was stationed at Culdrose in Cornwall Gary and I decided to go and see John Mayall's band in Plymouth, I think we hitched there and Glenn said we could stay the night at his place in Plymouth. Anyway, we went round to Glenn's and I said, "Thanks for the offer Glenn, but I think we'll hitch back to Culdrose."

Glenn said "I think you're both insane." And we probably were. John Mayall had formed a new line up for a band that didn't include a drummer and used acoustic guitars, in the end Gary and I managed to get in for nothing, as I think it was near to the end of the concert and the bouncer let us in for free. The LP by John Mayall at that time was called, 'Turning Point.'

There were also trials going on board the Eagle with a Phantom Jet. This was the most amazing aircraft I had ever seen. To give it extra thrust, it put on after burners, which meant that prior to it being catapulted off the ship, two flames burned out of its exhausts. As for the noise, deafening is the only the word that springs to mind and whenever it took off, the Flight Deck Chief, cleared everyone off the flight deck who was not wearing ear defenders. Everyone had to wear two pairs; these consisted of a small pair inserted into the ears and then another pair that were worn in the helmet all flight deck crew wore. This jet was amazing; it could take off and go straight up at a ninety-degree angle into the sky, unlike other aircraft that went higher at a lesser angle.

I dearly wanted to photograph this jet head on and as luck would have it, a photographer was on board; his job was to film the take off, of the Phantom. I put word round that I wanted to meet him and so we were introduced. I offered him a sip of rum and got my pictures, albeit on an instamatic camera.

When I met the photographer in the tot room, he said, "The movie camera I use shoots each frame as a still. This enables the boffins to analyse how the aircraft is performing."

The photographer had drunk some of his tot and I duly topped him up with some of mine, to which he remarked. "I've never had this much before."

"Thank you for helping me to get my pictures." I replied.

I later discovered there were ratings billeted directly below the flight deck and whenever the Phantom took off, it burned the ceiling above their heads. I bet there weren't many that wanted to sleep on the top bunk in that mess.

Shortly after this we were issued with new gasmasks. They had an inflatable seal and Pete and I were in the hangar, trying to inflate the seal. A voice announced over the intercom, "Put on your gasmasks. These gasmasks are self-inflatory." How this was achieved to this day, I have no idea.

We were also shown a suit, which we were supposed to wear to protect us against some gas or other. Pete and I weren't paying attention as we'd removed our gasmasks, got into the rear of the helicopter closed the door and chatted.

The Eagle then set sail for America. First of all we sailed to Norfolk in Virginia and en route I went along to the cable deck and watched as dolphins swam in the wake of the bows.

Once at Norfolk, Tony and I went ashore and met up with some American sailors who took us to their PX club, where we had our first taste of pizza.

Tony and I were on special duties; this meant we were able to go ashore whenever we wanted. Paddy and John (the chiefs in charge of the flight) had it so organised that all the routine servicing was done before twelve each day. This meant I was able to go ashore every day.

Once, as Tony and I went ashore we heard the following message being broadcast from an American ship. 'Liberty guys to glamorise, bad guys to the Sheriff's Office.'

Having found not much to do in Norfolk, Tony and I decided to go out to Virginia Beach. To do this we took some civvies out to the bus station, changed out of our uniforms and placed them in a bag in a locker and caught a bus out to the beach. It was brilliant.

Tony wore jeans, a shirt and a waistcoat (which the Americans called a vest). We went into a store and I saw some copies of Playboy Magazine and cried out to Tony. "Oi Tony! They've got Playboy magazine here."

"What's it cost?"

"About the same as it does in England." I replied.

To which a woman stared daggers at me and said. "Shame on you boy!"

Also there was a plaque on a wall, which commemorated where the first shot was fired in the American Civil War.

Tony and I tried out a few bars and we had to produce ID to prove we were 21, which was the legal age of drinking in the State of Virginia. The bars were so different from the pubs in England. They had a long bar, which had mini juke boxes dotted along them, plus there were also booths to sit in and each one also had in it, a mini juke box.

The most popular tune at the time was 'Bad Moon Rising' by Creedence Clearwater Revival. At other times Tony and I would sit on the beach, which seemed to go on for miles. We were approached by guys who said. "Are you English?"

"Yes."

"Can you talk to us?"

"What do you want us to say?"

"Anything. We just love your accents and why have you got a vest on with Jeans?"

Tony didn't understand, but when he realised what they were on about, he laughed. They then said, "What do you think about Prince Charles inauguration?"

"What!" We both exclaimed.

"You know, Prince Charles?"

"Not personally," I replied.

"Yeah well your queen inaugurates him this year."

I finally twigged it, "Oh you mean he becomes the Prince of Wales?"

"Yeah that's it."

"Not too fussed really."

Word spread around the ship, that it was possible to sell your blood in Norfolk. The previous day, Terry had done this and collapsed outside Woolworth's. I went along to the place with some friends and they had all finished donating whilst mine was still dripping out of my arm. Once finished I decided, after Terry had collapsed the previous day to have a glass of water. But they were in a hurry to leave and so I quickly followed them.

Everything seemed fine as I never collapsed and that afternoon I was swimming out at Virginia Beach, although I didn't use the arm that I'd had blood taken out of.

It was while we were out at the Beach that Tony and I met two girls, who said they'd take us to a drive in movie. We went back to one of the girl's houses, where they changed. The drive in was a totally new experience for Tony and I, although I really can't tell you what film we saw. But the girls did run us back to our ship.

All too soon we were back at sea and I discovered that Al Hart (one of the S.A.R. team) had bought a huge Zippo lighter.

It transpired that at the N.A.A.F.I. shop, for 6d (2p), one could fill up a lighter. So Al used to go along place 6d in the box and discreetly fill up his lighter, which probably took most of a tin of fuel to fill. Now the odd thing was that Al didn't smoke. He'd merely bought the lighter for a laugh. So that when someone pulled out a cigarette, he could say. "Would you like a light?" And then pull out this veritable flamethrower.

Our next port of call was Boston in Massachusetts. All the time in Virginia I'd been drinking slush. This was an icy drink and, as the name implies a flavoured slushy drink. But when I tried to do the same in Boston I practically lost my voice, this was due to the colder weather in Boston and my laryngitis pleased my messmates.

Once again, Tony and I were ashore, it was night and there were two girls sat on a bench and Tony said. "I think those two fancy us."

"Well, we'll go over and chat them up." "But I don't know what to say."

"It doesn't matter. We're in uniform, so they know we're English, so it won't matter what we say."

Having said that, we strolled over to them and I said. "Hello. We just thought we'd come and save you from the Boston Strangler."

That was it we were in. So much so, that my girl gave me some smelly spray, which she'd obtained for her boyfriend. Later that night, the girls had to go home and so we were walking them to the underground when another girl approached us and said. "Are you guys English?"

"Yes." We replied.

"Well there's a party out at Cambridge for all you English guys."

"Thanks." We replied as we took hold of a leaflet, explaining where the party was.

"Don't go there." The girls said. "It'll be full of drugs."

We said we'd meet the girls tomorrow and went off to the party. I immediately thought of Simon and Garfunkel, mainly because they'd mentioned Cambridge Square in one of their songs.

The party was run by a tall, thin, black guy called Mark. One guy chatted to me about a super group called; Crosby Stills and Nash, plus he was also into the Jeff Beck Band.

The party was so different from the atmosphere we'd left in Virginia, because at this party black and white people mixed and I mentioned this to Mark who replied with. "This is nothing when I normally throw a party I have all races and gays. I'm visiting some friends tomorrow, would you like to come with me, Smiler?"

"OK. I'll see if I can get a weekend pass."

I returned to the Eagle and next morning asked John and Paddy, for a weekend pass.

"Whom are you staying with?" They asked.

"Don't know. His first name's Mark."

"Right, we'll put down Mr Mark."

"Probably gay." Someone said.

Unfortunately Tony couldn't come ashore with me and so I took Dan instead.

At Mark's we got into a car and drove out to his friend's, where we had a meal. I was offered a bottle of beer, but couldn't manage to remove the top. I was then shown it was a screw top, I felt a complete fool.

When the food was served, we had corn on the cob, which had two spikes on the plate with it. This was the first time that I'd ever seen corn on the cob and so, I proceeded to pick out each individual piece of corn with the spikes. I was then shown what to do, which was to put a spike intro each end of the cob and gnaw at the corn.

Although I'd made a fool of myself, I'd really enjoyed my stay with Mark and the next day, I showed him round the ship. He was aghast as I showed him the various methods of making war. As for my messmates, they said that I'd met Jethro Tull; at least that was how I read their implications about Mark. I also met a girl at Mark's and we wrote to one another, but it never got any further.

Whilst in Boston, the ship organised a one-day trip to New York. That was quite spectacular, as I went up the Empire State building, United Nations building, and a broadcasting building, where I think I saw Jimi Hendrix. I found New York to be somewhat dark; perhaps this was due to having been at sea in an open space and then to be surrounded by skyscrapers.

I'd enjoyed my time in the States but as the ship sailed back to England most of the crew were very restless. In fact I walked up in the night to the flight deck and there were loads of other sailors doing the same, was this jet lag?

The older ratings moaned about this, saying there were too many JDs on the ship.

During this time there was no flying and routine maintenance was carried out on the aircraft. I was advised to go into the adjacent mess as a rating that I'd heard rumours about, was going to perform his after shower routine. The rumour was that his cock hung out of the bottom of his shorts. I stood and watched the tall white guy as he dusted himself down with talcum powder, grabbed hold of his cock and swung it around like a propeller. His cock was easily twelve inches long and it was lost in a cloud of talcum powder.

Once we got back to England we went on leave.

CHAPTER FIFTEEN

It was August 1969 and my two weeks leave had expired and I was due to return to my ship. So with my holdall packed full of clothes, my passport in my pocket and a single railway ticket to Gothenberg in Sweden, I bid my parent's farewell and departed from their flat in Golders Green. I wandered through the park and felt very pleased with myself, because at last I was escaping from the clutches of the Royal Navy. I'd chosen to travel to Sweden, thinking I would be able to obtain political asylum. The reason behind my thinking was that Sweden was neutral and was already sought out as a refuge by deserters from Vietnam. The thought of never being able to return to Britain never bothered me. I firmly believed that if Britain only wanted me as a sailor, then I didn't want them.

I travelled alone until I'd crossed the English Channel by ferry. Then it was on to a French train that would take me north to Sweden. I caught sight of a tall teenager, with long dark hair, carrying a rucksack. I approached him and said, "Excuse me, are you English?"

"Yes." He replied.

"Where are you going to?"

"Gothenberg, in Sweden."

"Brilliant so am I. Any chance we can travel together?" I asked. "Why not. My name's Chris."

"My name's Smiler." This was also what I really appreciated about hitching, whatever you said your name was, people adhered to. Plus it was the end of forever being told to get a haircut. What's more, I could put my hands in my pockets, whenever I liked.

Chris and I boarded the train and walked along the corridors. There appeared to be no open or communal carriages, as they were all partitioned off with seats for eight people and a corridor ran along the length of the carriage. We found an empty carriage and Chris slid back the door and said, "'Ere this'll do."

We placed our luggage on the overhead racks and Chris said, "Stretch out on that side and try and stop anyone coming in."

We stretched out on the seats and deterred anyone from joining us in the carriage. At last the train pulled out of the station and headed north towards Sweden.

Chris sat up and asked, "What are you going to Sweden for Smiler?"

"I've just deserted from the royal navy, so I thought I'd get political asylum in Sweden."

Chris smiled, "I don't think you'll have much chance of that mate. Where are you going to stay?"

"Blimey! I never thought of that" I paused, "Youth hostels or bed and breakfast. I suppose."

"Sounds a bit pricey. Tell you what; I'm camping so why don't you share my tent, until you sort something out that is."

"Thanks Chris. So what do you do, and why are you going to Sweden?"

"I'm a student and I have a girlfriend in Gothenberg."

Having kept the compartment to ourselves, we stretched out and managed to get some sleep. We were occasionally interrupted as other passengers tried to join us, but we fobbed them off and they used the small; pull out seats that were available along the corridor.

As we approached the German border the door was flung open and a uniformed man entered the compartment and said, "Passports please!"

As I handed over my passport I was terrified in case the man queried my occupation of *Government Service*, then all would be lost. I would be dropped off at the next station and no doubt handed over to the military police. Hence I was nervous every time my ticket and passport were inspected. As we entered Denmark and the last person checked my credentials, Chris looked across to me and said, "You're fine now, we're in Scandinavia. There'll be no more border checks. You've done it, you've escaped."

"Chris, you don't know how good this feels. If I go back I have to serve another nine years. That would do me in."

"Christ! That's a life time, why so long?"

"I signed on as a mechanician apprentice, which meant I had to sign on for twelve years straight, instead of the usual nine years, and three in reserve. It's something to do with the cost of my course."

"Nine years is long enough, and yet you say that you have nine years left to do. Why did you join in the first place?"

"This is going to sound really silly. I just wanted to see the world."

"Did you see it?" Chris eagerly asked.

"I've just returned from the States."

"Wow! I bet that was good."

"Actually the States was weird. But on the ship there was no escape. You know what I mean. Normally you finish work, you go home and then you go out."

"Yeah, sure."

"The problem was, the ship was my home."

We crossed the last expanse of water and arrived at Helsingborg, in Sweden. We noticed the train for Gothenberg would be arriving shortly and so to while away the time, we entered the station buffet and ordered an expensive coffee each. But as we sat down, what I thought was rather odd, for although the buffet looked no different from any other railway buffet, well, it was a lot brighter, but was otherwise deserted. It was the music that was playing which put me more in mind of Switzerland than Sweden, because it was accordion music.

Finally, we boarded the train for the last leg of our journey and as the train pulled out of the station, I looked out of the window. To my amazement I noticed the line was only a single-track. I deduced that there was not much rail traffic. Because whenever there was another track, it was merely to allow the trains to pass. I later discovered the single-track railway was just another example of Swedish frugality.

CHAPTER SIXTEEN

For me the Swedish railway was more like a giant model train set. I never said much to Chris as I just stared out of the window at the land flashing by. The houses, of which there didn't seem to be many, were made of wood which was painted in different colours and many of the houses had a flagpole alongside, flying either the Swedish flag or pennant. Perhaps the other residents were on holiday, as they had naked flagpoles.

I turned to Chris and said, "Not many people live in Sweden then?"

"No. The population of the whole country is less than the population of London. Actually, we're only seeing a small part of the country, it's massive."

The train arrived at Gothenberg as Chris and I left the carriage he swung his pack onto his back. I picked up my holdall and we walked out of the station into brilliant sunlight. All I noticed were the pale blue trams.

We made our way to the Tourist Information where Chris chose a campsite that was near to a tram route. Luckily where the tram terminated was but a few metres from the campsite. We headed towards a wooden shed with a window in it; this housed both the reception and a small shop. In front of it was an area, which had several benches and tables in it, and of a night it was lit up by a string of lights. As the shop also served hot dogs and hamburgers, the area served as both a meeting point and a place to eat.

Having booked in, Chris and I climbed the small grassy hill and I helped Chris to erect his tent. Which Chris had chosen to erect near to the bathroom and toilets. As I had no sleeping bag, Chris offered me a large blanket to sleep in. Once we'd settled in we meandered around the site. To the rear of the campsite were many conifers, which led through to a lake. Camped in amongst the conifers were a few people who by camping there, used the facilities of the campsite, which were superb and avoided paying camping fees. In the centre of the lake was an island and although I felt tempted to try and swim out to the island, I decided to leave it for another day.

There were several Englishmen on the campsite and so for the first night, Chris and I didn't venture into the town, but instead we made the acquaintance of the other campers. When Chris told the others I was a deserter from the royal navy, it met with mixed reactions. The main question was why I'd joined? I also bought a postcard from an attractive blonde girl in the kiosk to send home. When I licked the stamp, it tasted of strawberries.

Roger, who was one of the students staying there, was obviously a Batman fan, as he'd renamed Gothenberg, Gotham City. He also said that in the town was a University, which had an excellent students bar where the beer was cheap.

The next day a small wiry chap from Hull, called Billy said, "You need to buy a sleeping bag. I know a place in town and you should buy a rucksack and place a Union Jack on it. Then people will be able to tell from which country you come from. They may moan about Britain, in fact I had a lift with a German who said which towns he'd bombed in the Second World War. But at least you'll get a lift and the cheapest and best way to travel, is by hitching."

That night at the campsite Billy said, "The railway station serves an excellent breakfast."

The following morning a few of us set out for the station and breakfast. So as not to arise too much suspicion, we entered in small groups.

It was exactly as Billy had described. We paid one price and could eat as much as we liked. There was a good selection of food and was known as a smorgasbord. The Swedes only had a few slices of bread or a piece of cake, which they washed down with black coffee.

We, on the other hand, wandered along the self-service counter and selected cereals, cakes, various types of bread and eggs, which were all washed down with fruit juice, milk or coffee. I poured milk, which looked rather thick, over my cornflakes, but when I tasted it, I realised that it was sour milk which is very popular with the Swedish. The others told me to take another bowl of cereal and ensure that I poured proper milk over it.

Having eaten our fill we gathered outside and Billy was the last to appear. His belly was actually bursting from his small frame and pushing out from his granny T-shirt.

"Blimey! You've packed it away there, Billy." I said.

"Well, that'll do me for three days now!"

"Like the jacket, where'd you get it from?" I asked Billy as I felt the texture of his brown, well-worn leather jacket, which Billy was now forced to leave unzipped.

"Yeah, it is pretty nifty. I bought it second hand at the flea market in Amsterdam, last year." Billy proudly proclaimed. I then went with Billy who showed me where to buy a sleeping bag. It was superb as it was warm and damp proof.

As we wandered around the town I thought how attractive the Swedish girls were, but I never got round to chatting any up and we went to Liseberg. This is an amusement park and there were attractive blonde girls in abundance.

One night we decided to try out the students' bar at the University, Roger said, "We won't need a student's union card, as they will accept our passports as evidence of proof. As it would clearly states, *Occupation, Student.*"

My passport didn't state that but nevertheless, I decided to go with them and as we descended into the cellar bar. Only a few of our passports were checked. I'd got away with it, although Billy did say, "You'll be able to get a students union card in Athens."

The cellar bar was laid out like a German Beer Keller. Which meant it was well lit, had a bar at one end and everyone was seated at long tables. It was an enjoyable night and after that, money allowing, we quite often frequented the students' bar.

The camp site had visitors from around the world, some turned up in vans with the words, *Nord Kap,* emblazoned upon them. Others had trophies in the form of antlers on the van. I discovered that the 'Nord Kap', was the highest anyone could travel north in Europe and was a good vantage point for the midnight sun, which I'd arrived too late in the year to see. A group of English students arrived and one of them had a bad leg and was unable to leave the campsite. They'd also camped near to the bathrooms. This was not a good thing to do, as the person with the bad leg having nothing to do, timed the sequence of the flushing water in the pissoir. I believe he'd injured his leg whilst climbing in Norway. Also some Dutchmen arrived who were accompanied by a loud-mouthed American.

One day when Chris went to visit his girlfriend I decided not to join the others by taking the tram into town, instead I went for a swim. I put on my swimming trunks and a T-shirt, grabbed a towel and went to the back of the campsite towards the lake. I took off my T-shirt and lay on the ground in the sun and took in my surroundings and lay there until I felt hot enough to swim in the lake.

The water was a clear brown and contrasted with the green of the leaves on the trees. Swimming out to the island, felt different to swimming either in the chlorinated water of a swimming pool, or else in the salty sea, for this was fresh water. Having reached the island I noticed many of the girls were topless. I stayed for a while and then swam back.

I'd been at the campsite for about two weeks and things were getting a bit tense, as one of the students took umbrage about me using the students' bar at the University. Being September the campsite was beginning to empty and Billy said, "It'll start to get cold soon and so you should head south."

"Where to?" I asked.

"Go to Amsterdam. You'll be able to get a job there. You'll also need a tent. I'm leaving soon, so I'll sell you mine."

I was given a sheet of plastic to place over the tent in case it rained.

Billy and I journeyed into town, and he took me to a shop where I purchased a high pack, which was huge. It had an aluminium frame, a large main waterproof compartment, three outside pockets, and leather straps which were covered in a soft fabric. There was a padded part, which stretched across my back to make it comfortable to walk with. I also bought a map of Europe and a decent sized Union Jack, which I managed to stick onto the rear of the pack.

Billy added, "The Union Jack will help you to get lifts."

I approached the Dutchmen, hoping to procure a lift with them to Holland. "Sorry, but we have the American." They said, "We met when he was drunk, and when he is sober he is awful. We'd rather take you Smiler, but there is no room for you. Good luck with hitching."

So I packed my belongings in the high pack. There was a place on the top where I could strap on the tent and at the bottom was a separate bag, where I could fit in my sleeping bag. I strapped my holdall onto the main compartment and when I hoisted the hi-pack on, although it was very comfortable, because it towered over me, I looked like a pack on legs.

I bid my new found friends farewell. They wished me luck and I boarded the tram for the last time and went back to the railway station. From there I chose the road going south. I was really enjoying myself, to travel like this without anyone telling me what to do. Was this the right path to take?

CHAPTER SEVENTEEN

I walked along with my arm outstretched and my thumb erect, thinking about how gorgeous Swedish girls were and how enjoyable my time in Sweden had been, this had been my whole reason for joining the navy. If only I'd known that by joining the navy, I'd chosen the wrong path!

I hadn't gone far when a VW pick-up van stopped and the driver, who wore a dark peaked cap, overalls and had a dark bushy moustache said. "Where are you going to?"

"Amsterdam, for a job."

"Ah so. I myself am German."

I hoisted my hi-pack into the rear of the pick-up and joined the driver in the cab. "How come you're working here in Sweden?" I asked him.

"In Germany, everything is 'papa says', here, I am free to take up any occupation."

"The roads are pretty good here."

"Ah, but you haven't seen the autobahns then?"

I caught several lifts to Malmo and from there I caught the ferry to Denmark. Once again fortune smiled on me, as I managed to catch a lift in the Friday rush hour. A Volvo stopped; the driver looked at me and said.

"You are very lucky, as I work in Copenhagen, but I live in Assens, which is in the middle of Denmark, so you are welcome to travel with me to my destination."

Denmark appeared to be quite a small country and once we left the ferry, the Volvo driver dropped me off. It wasn't long before I managed to get another lift, but when I was dropped off, I decided to sleep, albeit rough. I found it easy to read the signposts because the map I'd purchased was written in the language of each individual country.

The following day the lifts went well and I was soon in Germany, where I was eventually picked up by a couple in a Citroen 2CV. As I sat in the spartan seats of the car, which I thought owed a lot to deck chairs, but was nevertheless comfortable. I was wondering where I would stay that night when the woman, who'd done most of the talking, turned to me and said, "Where will you stay tonight?"

"I have no idea; I just want to get to Amsterdam."

"Well I don't think you'll make Amsterdam tonight. So my brother and I wondered if you'd like to stay with us for the night?"

"That would be very nice, thank you." I replied, although up until that moment, I wrongly assumed that they were husband and wife.

I then had a closer look at them and I could see a resemblance. They both had blond hair, although the woman's hair was darker and their clothes were very conservative.

The car pulled up outside a large double fronted house, which had black wooden gables. All three of us entered the front garden through a gate that was the only break in an otherwise symmetrical wooden fence. As we walked up the path I was overawed by the splendour of the house, which as far as I could ascertain was somewhere in northern Germany.

I dropped my hi-pack in the hall, which was decorated in a tidy, but old-fashioned style. The man went upstairs whilst his sister beckoned me to follow her through to the kitchen, where we sat and talked.

The man returned and spoke to his sister who said to me, "Have you a tent?"

I thought that it was an odd question but I replied, "Yes."

"That's good, you see our grandmother will not allow you to stay in the house, but my brother will help you to pitch your tent in the garden and then I will give you something to eat. In the morning we will drop you off on a better road to take you to Amsterdam."

I thanked her and wondered what on earth the British had done to this kindly couple's grandmother in the second, or was it the First World War, or both? I quickly dispelled these thoughts from my mind and went to retrieve my hi-pack from the hall. It didn't take long before my newly acquired tent was pitched in their back garden. It reminded me of when I was a small boy and I'd camped out in my parents back garden with my brother.

What struck me as odd was that when my tent was erected, I was invited back into the kitchen and given food, which I washed down with coffee. The tiled kitchen had a clinical feel about it and I sensed that the house lacked homeliness, but then perhaps this was the grandmother's influence, as the brother and sister had been very hospitable.

The following morning I was lying in my tent thinking, how pleasant life was, when my thoughts were interrupted by a woman's voice saying, "Hallo, are you awake?"

"Oh . . . yes." I replied.

"Well if you like to get dressed, you can have a wash in the house and join us for breakfast."

It didn't take me long to wriggle out of the sleeping bag, pull on my jeans and T-shirt, put on my shoes and socks, wander dreamily into the kitchen and say, "Good morning."

I was shown where to have a wash and as I did, I took in the surroundings. The whole house seemed to be decorated in the same cold, clinical style and everything looked to be in its correct place. There were ornaments dotted about, which looked as if they were scared to move, in case they were punished for being out of place.

I enjoyed a breakfast of coffee, cold meat and bread, after which I packed away my tent and was driven to a good road for Amsterdam. I was retrieving my hi-pack from the boot of their car and had just hitched it up onto my back, when the man extended his arm and said, "Good trip."

"You and your sister have been most kind, thank you very much."

The woman was now standing next to her brother and said, "It's nothing, and you're welcome."

They returned to their car and as they drove off, the woman gave a friendly wave, which I returned and they were gone.

CHAPTER EIGHTEEN

I reached Amsterdam on Sunday lunchtime and I could not believe my eyes, because the place was alive with people. This was a complete contrast to London, which then was a fairly sedentary place.

I found the Tourist Information, which was open and after enquiring about a camp site took a tram to a little way out of the centre to Olympiad, where the campsite was. The main form of transport in Amsterdam appeared to be bicycles or trams. At the campsite I booked in, quickly erected my tent, took any valuables with me and headed straight back into town.

That first day I was happy to saunter around and sample the Amsterdam way of life. I ambled around the myriad of streets and squares, investigating them to try and ascertain what Amsterdam had to offer. There were numerous shops selling a variety of things. I was fascinated by the record stalls, which had LP covers hanging around them. I also discovered that there were two main squares, Rembrandtsplein and Leidseplein, the latter being colloquially named by a fellow tourist, Led Zeppelin, after the rock band of the era.

For my first week in Amsterdam I just familiarised myself with the outlay of the city and also to look for work. I discovered to my delight that there were two breweries and they both offered guided tours, which fortunately were on different days.

First I took the tour around the Amstel Brewery, which as I went round with the others; the guide explained the intricacies of brewing beer. As we passed the huge vats of beer, I inhaled the odour and found it to be rather unpleasant. The tour culminated in the group being shown to a cellar, to sample the beer, which for many others and I was the main point of the tour.

We were shown to a long table where we were all promptly served with a beer and to help us drink the beer, there were a few snacks placed upon the table. As soon as any of us had finished a glass of beer, it was replaced with another one. In this way several beers were drunk and everyone got to know each other.

Later in the week I sampled the Heineken Brewery. The guided tour was similar to the Amstel Brewery, but the 'tasting' was not as good. There was nothing to eat, and one was not continually topped up with beer; instead a few beers were handed out, but on both the tours I made some good friends and established how to get a job.

My finances were low and so I approached a waiter, who was outside a cafe wiping tables and I said, "Excuse me, do you speak English?"

The waiter stood proudly erect and replied, "In Amsterdam, we all speak English!"

"Oh that's good. Is there any chance that I could have a job here please?"

The waiter smiled and said, "Sorry, we have nothing at present. Why not try the hotels?"

I thanked the waiter and headed for Rembrandtsplein and the Hotel American, where after a few enquiries I was employed as a dishwasher. I had to start at six in the morning and work through to four in the afternoon. It was a six-day week and Sunday was to be my day off.

My next task was to find out what time the trams started and seeing an authoritative looking man in a uniform at the tram stop. I approached him and said. "Excuse me. But what time do the trams start in Amsterdam?"

The man looked at me, and with an authoritative, cocksure voice he replied, "In Amsterdam, the trams all start early."

"OK." I said, calling his bluff, "What time do they start then?" "Six in the morning!" Came his curt, pompous reply.

I thanked him but thought how useless it was, as it meant I would have to walk to work. This entailed rising at 4.00am, dressing, washing and walking to the hotel.

As I arrived on my first morning and entered via the staff door, the doorman who looked resplendent in his uniform greeted me.

Feeling very Dutch I replied with, "Morgen," because that's what it sounded like to me. It met with a smile of approval from the doorman.

I then entered the depths of the hotel and reported to the man in charge. Whereby I was introduced to the monster known as, the 'Dishwashing Machine.'

It was situated in the middle of the room and the majority of the workers were Moroccan. The 'machine' was very inefficient and spewed out water and all the crockery and cutlery had to be dried by hand. I stripped down to a T-shirt and still the sweat poured from me. It was the hardest work I'd ever done. The young Arab boy, who worked alongside me, kept telling me not to rush. This seemed stupid to me, as then the dishes just piled up.

To the front of the 'Machine' was a raised platform, where very dark Moroccans stood, wearing orange aprons over their clothes and they also wore wellington boots. Their job was to clean the enormous pots and pans.

All the workers were friendly and for the first break in the morning, we were offered cheese and bread. I watched as the Moroccans sprinkled bits of chocolate on the cheese. They gesticulated that I should try it which I did, and found it to be a pleasant taste.

After the break I was taken to a room that had chairs placed at one end of it, they'd presumably been put there to allow someone to vacuum the hall. I was then shown where to place the chairs. It was a welcome relief from washing dishes.

There was also a Japanese youth, who would sing a pop song, which I'd only known as Sukiyaki and was sung by Kyu Sakamoto. It had been released in England in the mid-sixties. The Japanese boy did not stay long, as he said that Holland was too expensive.

At the end of my working day I caught the tram home, I'd been advised to buy a block of tickets, which was in fact a piece of cardboard with red stripes on it. Each time I entered the tram, I stuck the ticket in a franking machine, which stamped the time and the day onto a red strip on the card. This allowed me to use any tram for a certain amount of time to reach my destination.

Back in my tent I just flopped out and fell asleep. Sometimes I slept right through to the following day. Other times I would lie there in a trance like dream until I was rudely awakened by a police siren echoing out across the streets. This sent a chill through my body as I thought, 'Are they coming for me?'

If I wasn't too tired I sampled the disco, which before a certain time had a free entrance. This meant I would have to buy a drink and when this was empty, whenever the waiter approached and asked if I wanted a drink I replied, "I'm just going to have a dance."

It was easy to familiarise myself with the streets and canals of Amsterdam, and so I never needed to take a boat tour around the canals, as I walked round most of them.

On some evenings I dropped into the youth hostel and it was there that I was advised to see a film called 'Easy Rider'. For some time I'd been intrigued by posters that showed a man wearing a leather jacket, on the back of which was emblazoned the flag of the Stars and Stripes. The words underneath the man said in English,

"This man came to look for America!"

Unbeknown to me these posters were advertising the film, Easy Rider. The student said, "In Holland, all films are shown in their original language, with Dutch subtitles".

Thus enlightened I went to see Easy Rider. I thoroughly enjoyed it and could sympathise with Billy and Captain America, the heroes of the film.

One morning I left my tent for the usual walk to work, but outside the walls of the campsite I noticed how foggy it was and I got lost. I came to a crossroads and instead of walking straight on, I turned right.

When I heard the gong of a tram rumbling down the centre of the road, I realised my dilemma. Not only was I lost but also, I was late for work.

I arrived half an hour late for work and was severely reprimanded. In the afternoon of that day a stocky, grey haired man approached me and said, "Come with me please."

I immediately thought the worst, and assumed that I was to be sacked. Instead I was led upstairs and given a different job. Prior to entering a darkened room the man said,

"You good worker, you get more money!"

I thought to myself, 'Yes, I've heard that one before, but nothing ever came of it.'

I adjusted my eyes to the darkness of the windowless room. There was a table in the room, at which was sat a portly, white haired lady, dressed in dark clothes. The man gesticulated for me to be seated, he then left and the portly lady showed me what to do.

It was quite simple, all I had to do, was to polish the cutlery. It was so much easier than washing dishes and instead of standing for most of the day at the 'Machine', I was now able to sit down and work.

The lady spoke good English and close to, she was younger than I first thought she was. The darkness of the room, from a distance, made her look quite old. It was then that I noticed she had hardly any lines on her face, and what I had misconstrued as white hair, was actually blonde.

It was a pleasant afternoon's work and to my utter amazement, the following week, I had an increase in pay but I was still sweating it out on the 'Machine'.

I made the most of my Sundays off work and having gradually got to know Amsterdam, I began to enjoy the city. It was not very large, well not by London's standards and the main form of transport was bicycle, although I thought that pedalling along the cobbled streets would not make for the most comfortable of rides. The funniest thing I observed, were the couples that left the discos on mopeds. The guys drove whilst the girls sat precariously perched upon the rear mudguard, or else a very uncomfortable looking carrier with their legs dangling down.

One day I stood in awe, as what I thought was a solid bridge straddling the canal rose up in the air with all its tramlines and tram wires intact. The barge had its funnel tilted over to allow it to sail under the low bridges, and so it floated along oblivious to the traffic that had stopped for it.

At other times I just sat and watched as the heavily laden barges, chugged along the canal. Of course there were the tourist boats, where people stared out from beneath a glass canopy, whilst the guide prattled on in different languages.

Alongside the canals, there were a great many houseboats, which were all brightly painted and many of them had plants on the deck and several had the obligatory bicycle stowed on board.

There was one place I took a great delight in visiting. I saw a postcard upon which was a picture of a very old bridge. After much searching I found it. From this viewpoint, I could observe Amsterdam from a distance. There was a church that had many bells in it and when they rang out, it was not like the boom of 'Big Ben' in London.

It was a gentle sound, as if a group of campanologists were ringing the bells. In fact most of the bells throughout Amsterdam rang out with

THE WRONG PATH

a gentle tinkling sound as opposed to a large booming drone, which is so familiar with English church bells.

At one time during my ambles around Amsterdam I saw a sign in a doorway which wanted American or western European passports. I presume they were for illegal immigrants. I thought about selling mine but when I went to declare it stolen, I've no doubt that I'd be handed over to the military and so I decided to hang on to my passport. Mind you on hindsight, it might have been funny to see whoever bought the passport being questioned by the immigration authorities and handed over to the military police.

I'd worked in Amsterdam for a little over a month; I studied my resources, they looked good, plus, I'd bought a small radio and a jacket. I decided to hand in my notice and move on. My last day's work was on a Saturday but for me, one day was as good as another for travelling.

The day after I'd finished work I went into the workers dining area for food to make up some sandwiches for the journey. My fellow workers had informed me that I could pop in on my day off, to get something to eat, but this was the first time I'd taken advantage of it.

A well-dressed, dark haired, stern looking man challenged me. I gave him my name, knowing it was a Sunday he would not be able to find out anything until the following day, by which time I didn't know if I'd still be in Holland, let alone Amsterdam!

Having eaten I returned to the campsite, took down my tent, packed everything into my hi-pack and swung it onto my shoulders. I looked down to where my tent had stood, and there was now a rectangle of yellow/white grass. That was all that remained of my stay in Amsterdam. I settled my bill for camping, took one cursory glance at the few remaining tents. I wore a T-shirt, jeans, my new Dutch jacket, and my desert boots.

I hitched north through Holland and it was the first time I'd seen windmills, for which Holland is so renowned. The houses looked very elegant and were made of brick, and although I enjoyed the scenery I found it to be very flat.

I had been stood outside a house for some time trying to hitch a ride, when a slim redheaded girl appeared at the gate and said, "Excuse me, are you English?"

I turned to face her and said, "Yes."

"Would you like to come inside for something to eat?" She asked. "Yes." I replied and followed her down the steps and along the path into the house. I left my hi-pack in the hall and went into the front room, which was very English in its decor.

A grey haired bespectacled man, wearing a suit, looked up from his armchair and said, "As it is four o'clock and you're English, we thought you'd like to join us for some tea."

How typically English, I thought, everything stops for tea at four. Seated on their sofa this brought a smile to my face.

"You can have some soup, bread and meat. After which, my daughters will drive you to a better place for a lift." The man took a sip of his tea and continued, "Where are you heading for?"

"Sweden." I replied, thinking that this time I would apply for political asylum, because at that moment I couldn't believe how kind people were. First there had been the German brother and sister, now there was this Dutch family. As I was sat in their front room, staring out of the window and up to the road, I thought I could have easily been in a village in England.

At that moment my thoughts were disturbed as the man's wife entered the room carrying a tray, upon which was a bowl of soup, together with some bread and meat. I ate the light meal, taking my time not wishing to be in a hurry, in case I appeared to be ungrateful. After a while I thanked the man and his family for their hospitality and his daughters led me out to a car and dropped me off at a better place for hitching a ride.

"Good trip." They said as they left in their car.

"Thank you and please thank your parents again for the food." The girls turned their car round and drove back to their house. I thought to myself, I still have the sandwiches from the hotel but then, there's always tomorrow.

That night I hadn't gone very far and remained in Holland, sleeping in a field, which overlooked a canal.

CHAPTER NINETEEN

It was very early in the morning when I arrived at the border. I left the Dutch section and ambled through to the German section, where I was stopped and challenged by the border guard.

"Passport please!"

I pulled the passport out of my pocket and meekly handed it to the guard, who studied it and said. "Come with me please!"

I was scared stiff, I felt that my newly found freedom was about to come to a drastic end. This was because my job was listed as *Government Service*, which at the time provoked comments like, *"they'll think you're James Bond"*. But this guard knew the meaning of those words and I felt that soon, I would be picked up by the army and then returned to Britain as a deserter. It was the worst feeling I'd ever known.

The guard lead me inside a building and halted outside an empty office fortunately, his superior officer was not in attendance. He stabbed a finger at the passport where my job was listed as, *Government Service*.

"Vot is dis?" He asked.

With relief I replied, "Me luftwaffe," which I followed by making the sound of a gun going off, then bent over and held my stomach, as if I was in agony and added, "Injured, so left luftwaffe."

THE WRONG PATH

The border guard stood to attention, handed me back my passport and saluted.

I thanked him and was so relieved that I couldn't wait to leave Germany and enter Denmark, only then would I once again be free. Having no watch it occurred to me that I was lucky to have made such an early start to my travels that day, but the experience I felt at the border, is not one I would like to repeat.

Fortunately, there were no more incidents like that and once in Denmark I thought I'd return via Helsingor in Denmark, to Helsingborg in Sweden, the reason being that it was the cheapest route. At that time to cross Denmark which is basically a series of islands meant having to board a ferry from the west of Denmark, just past Odense to the north east of Denmark to where I was heading, Helsingor. I could've crossed from Copenhagen into Sweden but that meant using a ferry which would cost me money, whereas the one into Helsingor was free. The rides had gone well and I kept on hitching into the night, as I wanted to try and make the border that night and perhaps spend the night in Sweden.

It was late in the night when a VW Beetle driven by a thin man in his twenties, with shoulder length blond hair stopped and offered me a lift. Once we were on our way, he said. "Tell me, would you like some tea and possibly something to eat?"

As it had been a long while since I'd eaten my sandwiches from the Dutch Hotel I eagerly replied, "Yes."

We drove up to a wooden house which wasn't far from the ferry to Sweden. He parked his car and we climbed to the top of the stairs of the building. When he'd unlocked the door to the flat I placed my hi-pack on the floor. The Dane turned on a pale yellow light that was sufficient for me to absorb my surroundings.

While I stood there taking it all in the Dane filled an old kettle and placed it on a gas ring. The room had no wallpaper only the unpainted walls of pinewood. Upon one wall there were bookshelves but the books were not placed tidily as in a library, but were lying higgledy-piggledy. On the floor was a low, square table.

The Dane said, "Please, sit down make yourself comfortable."

I sat on a soft, very comfortable seat whilst the Dane placed a pot of tea and some large cups on the table followed by a plate of bread and meat. Then he extracted an LP from its sleeve and placed it on an old record player from out of which exuded the sounds of Bob Dylan.

Wearing jeans, a dark jacket and a light brown shirt, the Dane looked the epitome of a mature student. He poured us both a cup of tea and as he added no milk I gave him a quizzical look.

This he noticed and sat down saying, "I know you English like your tea with milk but please, try it the Danish way."

I raised the large cup to my lips and thought it resembled a soup bowl rather than a cup; perhaps these cups were where the expression, 'A dish of tea,' arose from. What's more the tealeaves at least by English standards were enormous and, the taste although pleasant, was not like any tea I'd tasted in England. I replaced the cup on the table and took a sandwich.

"This tea is very different from the tea I'm used to. But I like it." I said.

For a fleeting moment the Dane smiled and replied, "All you need is music, a good book, food in your belly and something to drink."

I could easily have spent the night chatting away but after several cups of tea and many sandwiches, I made my excuses and left. The house as I've already stated, was but a short walk away from the ferry and as I passed through the ticket office I looked up at the clock it was almost midnight.

For the second time in my life I had once again arrived on Swedish soil. I walked out of the town towards the main road and searched for a place to sleep. I pulled out my sleeping bag and once again slept in a field.

The following morning I decided to head for Stockholm and the rides went well until I was in a VW Karman Ghia, which was involved in a crash. Although neither the driver nor myself were injured, there was some minor damage to the car. The VW driver blamed the other driver saying,

"I've got my lights on! What's the matter with him?"

I almost expected him to say, *blithering idiot*. But then I was not in England. The driver asked for my address in case he needed me as a witness, so I gave him my parents' address in England.

After that hazardous ride I got a lift with some labourers who took me to a quarry where they gathered their belongings. They informed me that their job was to blast the rock which then went into the manufacture of railway chippings. Having left the quarry we arrived at a small town and I was offered the spare bed in their room for the night.

The room itself was quite spartan and resembled a dormitory. I deposited my pack there and we went for a meal. I'd changed my money earlier that day, into Swedish Krones. Having eaten, the labourers scanned the papers for a film and they chose one called 'Eva'.

Although the film was in Swedish I had no problem in understanding what it was about, as it was more like a blue movie as Eva's clothes kept coming off.

The following morning prior to going to work the labourers left me at a good vantage point for hitching a ride. Arriving in Stockholm I decided to stay in the youth hostel, which oddly enough, was situated on an old sailing ship.

One of the attendants on the ship was English, he was tall, had brown hair, was heavily built and offered me some advice. "Look mate, it's gonna get really cold here soon. I was thinking of going to Israel to work on a Kibbutz." He pulled out a handkerchief, blew his nose and continued, "Okay, so it'll take you awhile to get there, but it won't cost you anything as you can hitch overland. You won't need any food, as eventually somebody will feed you."

"Sounds like a good idea I'll think about." I replied.

I decided not to go to Israel as it would mean having to once again travel through Germany and as the youth hostel was working out to be expensive, I decided to look for cheaper accommodation. Asking around I found a place that offered cheap accommodation for students and immigrants and the adverts were in English.

Me at base of mast HMS St Vincent

HMS Collingwood living block

Beds made up as laid down in Admiraly
Instructions HMS Collingwood

Me No1 uniform HMS Collingwood

Passport photo 1967

Me HMS Seahawk shaved my head

Me Deserter Sweden

Me awaiting trial by court martial

Me awaiting trial by court martial 2

Me out of navy

CHAPTER TWENTY

So it was that I entered a somewhat derelict part of Stockholm. The buildings looked ancient and were made of wood. There was a small amount of paint on the wood, but even that was flaking off the wooden houses. I checked the address I'd written down, approached the house and knocked on the door.

It was opened by a thin, gaunt man, whose skin was stretched tautly over his face, giving his head a skull like appearance, what hair he had, was white and his dark, shiny suit, hung on him as if he were a coat hanger. In fact he wouldn't have looked out of place in a *Hammer House of Horror* movie.

Having announced myself, I followed him upstairs to his flat and we entered a room, where there was very little space as most of the floor was covered with camp beds.

The man looked at me and said, "You can pay half rent if you like."

Being fascinated, I enquired about it. The man then led me through to a room where there was only one bed; apparently half rent meant sharing the bed with the landlord.

I declined the offer; I wasn't that hard up, or gay. He showed me a camp bed; I removed any valuables from my hi-pack and returned to the centre of Stockholm.

Whilst walking round a grass square, I noticed a large hotel that appeared to be guarding a corner of it. I approached the hotel and inquired about a job, hoping this time I could become a bellboy.

The woman who interviewed me, had light brown, shoulder length hair, and wore a figure hugging, woollen trouser suit. She looked stunning.

Once again, I was employed as a dishwasher but what I hadn't realised was, that if I'd stayed at the front of the hotel, I could've become a bellboy but as I was at the rear of the hotel, I'd reverted to being a dishwasher. I didn't realise that in Sweden the length of hair didn't matter, as mine hadn't been cut since I left the navy and I had a stigma about it, hence I went round the back of the hotel for a job.

When I started work the conditions were so much better than those in Amsterdam, the dishwasher was superb as it was merely a case of placing the items in the racks provided, where they then entered the machine and as they emerged on the other side, all I had to do was to lift them off. An elderly man, whose blond hair was turning white, told me to leave the dishes and cutlery. I took his advice, as I thought he was in charge but by leaving the dishes and cutlery it allowed them to dry.

The entire hotel staff were given a uniform and the elderly man who was telling me what to do, although he was a bit podgy, still looked very dapper in his uniform.

For meals, there was also the addition of a glass of beer and at the end of work I made full use of the excellent shower facilities.

At lunch one day I was introduced to a man who had well groomed hair; a neatly trimmed beard and wore a light brown suit, as he was English I asked him.

"Do you have any plans to return to England?"

"I don't think so." He replied, "I enjoy my job, I can go ski-ing and then of course, there are the women!"

"Yes." I replied, "They are gorgeous."

My heart jumped with joy perhaps living in Sweden wouldn't be so bad after all. But all this changed when I was called into the office and was asked for my work permit. As I had none I had to leave the job.

I was thrown into turmoil, as I had no idea what to do. It was November and I was stuck in a strange country with no work and knew that eventually my money would expire, but never the less; I decided to have a look around Stockholm.

In one square there was a large sign erected which said, 'Eat Swedish Apples'. As it was written in Swedish I got someone to translate it for me, and it was then that I discovered that the sign was made up entirely of apples.

In Store Plan I thought I'd stumbled across a roadwork's, but I was wrong. For although there were roadwork signs around part of the square, at the centre was a statue of a man emerging from a manhole.

I also discovered a good bar called Store Hof and like Amsterdam there was a disco, which before a certain time allowed people in for nothing. There were two DJ's who worked on alternate nights and on one particular night the English DJ, at the end of a session played The Beatles Abbey Road Album in its entirety. As it had only just been released, it was the first time that I'd heard it and I was not impressed with it. Although the disco was pleasant, warm and free.

I then started working in the evening for a company that required English speaking people. The other workers were great, but as I had to sell encyclopaedias on a commission only basis I made no sales, and earned nothing.

I once again felt very despondent, but the girls that worked there were very helpful and bought me coffee and snacks. I remember one apartment that I went into, the couple didn't speak very good English and so they handed me over to their daughter and we just chatted about music. She put on an LP by Creedence Clearwater Revival and asked me where I went. I mentioned the disco where I'd heard the Abbey Road LP. I left saying I'd see her there.

One evening before we set out to try and sell encyclopaedias, the boss said that we had to wait for Grogan. Who, or what Grogan was, I had no idea of.

When Grogan arrived, I discovered that he was an Englishman from Dunstable, he was about the same height and age as me, but he was thinner and had short mousy hair and wore a dark blue suit, with a double-breasted jacket.

Having made Grogan's acquaintance, I discovered that his name was Peter and I told him my plight.

To which he replied, "It'll be difficult for you to obtain political asylum. If you really want to stay in Sweden, your best bet is to marry a Swedish girl. I don't know about you Smiler, but selling encyclopaedias is getting me nowhere."

"I'm like you." I glumly replied, "I turn up at the office of a night and that's it, I never make a sale but I don't know what to do."

"I think I'll quit this job, so how would you like to come back with me to Gothenberg? Brigit and I, she's my wife, will try and find you a job."

Feeling so happy I could've jumped for joy, and so naturally I replied, "Yes."

We both spent an unfruitful evening trying to sell encyclopaedias and then went off with two girls, one of whom said she was engaged to Lee Kirslake, who was the drummer of Uriah Heep. We left the girls and Peter drove me to my flat in his VW Beetle. I never went back to the disco nor did I see that girl who liked Creedence Clearwater Revival, again.

As we entered the room Peter could not believe his eyes. We clambered over the sleeping bodies and I informed the landlord that I was leaving. As I paid him on a weekly basis I owed him no rent, just grabbed my belongings and left.

CHAPTER TWENTY ONE

We drove through the night to Gothenberg and stopped en route for something to eat and to give Peter a break from driving.

In between mouthfuls of food I asked Peter. "Won't your wife mind me staying with you?"

"It'll be all right." He replied.

"How did you meet her?"

"She was an au pair in England. We dated she got pregnant, so I married her."

"But why live in Sweden?"

"Thought I'd try it out."

"How're you getting on?"

"Not bad could be better." He replied as we left the café.

At Gothenberg Peter headed out to a suburb called Vastra Frolunda, we pulled up outside a block of flats removed our belongings from the Beetle and wandered over to the entrance of one of the block of flats. Peter spoke into the entry phone, the door opened we entered and waited for the lift to arrive.

Entering Peter's flat he said, "Leave your pack in the hall and can you take your shoes off? It's a Swedish thing."

As we entered the living room Peter said, "Brigit this is Smiler he'll be staying with us for a while."

"Hey Smiler," she said.

"Hello Brigit." I replied as I looked into her blue eyes but otherwise to me she didn't look Swedish as she was short and had long dark hair.

"You have a sleeping bag?" Peter asked.

"Sure."

"Good you can sleep in the kitchen, as you can see this place is small but it has everything. It's late so we'll go to bed. Unfortunately the sofa is being used as a bed so we'll talk in the morning"

The following morning I got up and dressed and Brigit asked, "Would you like a cup of tea and something to eat?"

"Yes please the tea would be most welcome, but I thought you drank coffee."

Brigit smiled, "As you and Peter are English we will have tea."

Brigit served the meal saying, "Do you have any washing Smiler?"

"Yes."

"Leave it over there and I'll wash it. We have in the basement a washing machine and drying room."

The flat although not very large had some very modern amenities. These comprised of a living room, a bedroom, where the baby slept and a kitchen which incorporated a fridge, freezer, cooker and hob, over which was a fume extractor. Plus the flat was centrally heated by radiators and had double-glazing throughout.

The first night I was there we hadn't long finished eating when we were visited by two lissom blonde girls who both chatted away eagerly in English. Once they had gone Peter said. "They're schoolgirls, they're only thirteen."

I was amazed because to me they looked a lot older. After that initial visit the girls became regular visitors and they probed me with all sorts of questions.

"We like seeing you Smiler as it makes change from Frolunda Tory." This was a reference to what at the time was the first European shopping mall I made them cups of coffee that they had in small cups and asked them "As you drink so much coffee why is it served in such small cups?"

"The large cups are for tea."

The coffee was thick and black but I got used to drinking it the Swedish way. The girls used to keep saying va, which I found out meant what. They used to say en gong til a lot, this I found out meant say again.

On another night a very attractive blonde arrived. She had short blonde hair and her name was Maude, she spoke in Swedish to Brigit and then to me and she said, "I'm Agnetha's older sister."

Agnetha was one of the schoolgirls who had a crush on me. Oddly enough Peter was seldom there I got on very well with Brigit and often ribbed her about her English accent. I would ask her "What do we have to eat?"

"Soap."

"Soap," I replied, "but you wash with that". She meant soup. She got her own back, "Say cheese in Swedish."

"Oost," I replied.

"We have east to eat then. See you not so clever."

Brigit read the paper and said, "I've found a job for you Smiler."

"What is it?"

"A window cleaner."

"Makes a change from dish washing."

She made a phone call and said, "You can start at half before seven on Monday. Peter will show you where it is."

Peter took me to where the place was in the city centre and said, "That's where it is you can catch a tram on Monday. Just buy a pack of tickets and stamp one each time you use it."

"That's the same as Amsterdam." I replied.

"Right let's go for a sauna." Peter said as we drove off, "have you ever had a sauna?"

"No."

As we drove along to the sauna Peter said, "This'll be an experience for you, but why did you join the navy Smiler?"

"To travel but I've really enjoyed these past few months."

"So what'll you do now?"

"Like I said in Stockholm I thought perhaps, I'd be able to get political asylum."

Peter smiled, "Nice try but as you joined of your own free will by all means apply as it will allow you stay here and work, in the end they will say no. Your best bet is to marry a Swedish girl."

"I must say that they are very attractive."

We entered a building put our clothes in a locker and went naked into a hot room where there were blokes seated. The sweat was pouring out of my body and after a while Peter said, "Come on let's have a shower."

In the shower the other blokes said, "Are you English?"

"Yes."

"Do you have a cold shower after sauna?"

"No." I replied.

"You not a viking."

After that I always followed a hot shower with a cold one.

CHAPTER TWENTY TWO

My first day of work as a window cleaner arrived and starting so early in the morning; I thought I'd easily get a seat on the tram, but I was wrong. The tram was full of people also travelling to work and as a consequence I stood for most of the tram ride. I got off the tram and made my way to the address of the window cleaning office, where I descended down some steps into darkness. The boss was an elderly man and he introduced me to his son Bjorn, who spoke very good English.

"Good morning, I am Bjorn." The son said as he shook my hand."

"I'm Smiler."

"Good, you start work at half before seven and finish at four, but Friday is half day."

Although it was only a menial job the wages were good; well they were compared to wages in England at the time.

After I'd been working for a while we stopped for a break and went to a store that had a café and the two main workers gave me a Donald Duck magazine and said. "Read this."

I looked through it and they said, "Read it out loud." Being in Swedish I tried my best.

"You understand?" They asked.

"No."

"You read this and you don't understand. You crazy!" They said laughing.

Every now and again I would say to Bjorn, "This is a bit tricky."

But he didn't understand what I was saying and I told him to ask his sister who apparently spoke very good English, he never did, because he thought that I was swearing.

After work that night I said to Peter, "How come the tram was so full that early in the morning?"

"The whole of the Volvo factory start work between six and seven in the morning."

"Even the office workers?"

"Yes, everyone in Sweden starts work early and that means the Swedish also go to bed early, normally around nine o'clock at night."

One evening whilst waiting for the tram to take me home I noticed a lot of young men stood in the queue who were wearing caps with a shiny peak and a soft top, which tapered to a tassel that hung over one side of their head. I later discovered that they were graduation caps.

If it was at all possible I believed that I was turning Swedish. For a start I hadn't cut my hair since I'd left England which was in August and so as my hair is naturally curly, I looked like a cross between Jimi Hendrix and Eric Clapton. What's more I'd even bought an ice hockey jersey, which was yellow and had black hoops round it.

Of a night I would watch the television with Brigit. The television programmes were in the original language with Swedish sub-titles and as most of the programmes were from either America or Britain, I could easily understand them. Actually I'd learnt how to ask for a stamp for a letter to England; it was something like, "Femty fem ure freemaker." This translates as a 55 ure stamp and I could also say hello and window cleaner in Swedish.

Brigit smiled as she said, "You speak Swedish with a Finnish accent."

"At least people won't think I'm English."

But Finnish they drink too much." She replied.

One day Brigit picked up the paper and said, "Why don't you take Agnetha to see this film?"

It was called 'The Language of Love' the film was a typical Swedish film where hardly anyone kept their clothes on.

Maude said, "Agnetha has a crush on you."

"Brigit suggested I take her to see the film, 'The Language of Love', but I'm not sure." "Why not?"

"Well the film's about . . . ."

"Smiler this is Sweden, we know all about that." Maude interrupted me.

As for Agnetha yes she was very attractive but as she was only thirteen I thought to myself, I'm not exactly Jerry Lee Lewis who had actually married his thirteen-year-old cousin.

In the end Peter and I went to see the Wild Bunch and it was brilliant.

Some days I would either walk around the shopping mall, or else walk around the surrounding area, which led to a sports field that was near to the flats.

CHAPTER TWENTY THREE

It was starting to get colder and as I'd been working for a few weeks I said to Brigit one Thursday night, "I won't be home tomorrow afternoon as I'm going to Denmark to buy a Scandinavian ski coat."

Having finished at lunch time on Friday I hitched down to Malmo and caught the ferry across to Denmark. I chose that route as it was the nearest to Copenhagen, where I believed I would have the best opportunity of purchasing a coat. I chose Denmark as it was something to do and also the coats were cheaper than in Sweden.

I wandered around the market looking for a leather ski coat but couldn't find one small enough, at the time I weighed nine stone ten pounds about sixty one kilos. In the end I bought a canvass ski coat that had the obligatory sheepskin lining and it certainly did the job of keeping me warm. Having got what I came for I hitched back and even though it was late when I arrived at Gothenberg I still managed to catch a tram to Vastra Frolunda, apparently Gothenberg operates a nightly tram service.

The following Monday we were cleaning the windows of a large store and afterwards had a free breakfast and as we sat down, one of the guys said to me.

"What did you do at the weekend?"

"After work on Friday, I hitched down to Copenhagen to buy a ski coat."

"Did you buy one? And why did you go to Copenhagen?" He asked. "You can buy them in Sweden."

"I'd been told about the flea market in Copenhagen and I thought they'd be cheaper, which as they were second hand they were. So I bought one. Also it was something to do."

"Was it skin?" He asked, meaning leather.

"No." I replied.

I was working near to the railway station and as I went about my task of cleaning windows, I noticed a shop selling hand carved trolls and thought they would make an ideal gift for my parents. The one I really fancied was a forked twig which had trolls climbing all over it, but it was too expensive and so instead I bought a man and woman troll in a rowing boat and as the oars were detachable it made it easier to post.

Sometimes of a weekend I would try out the discos and I also managed to see Fleetwood Mac and Ten Years After. It was just so good to see some English bands. Fleetwood Mac performed the song, 'Oh Well', I just loved it.

I arrived home from work one night and Brigit said, "Your boss phoned and told me you will get a rise."

This I did not believe but yet again I did get a rise and it led to being in charge of a Norwegian who had just started and spoke very little English. This was odd as I spoke very little Swedish, let alone Norwegian.

It was getting near Christmas and the boss of the window-cleaning firm had often asked Brigit where my work permit was? Things were beginning to look a bit shaky and Peter said, "To obtain a work permit, you will have to leave Scandinavia."

"But I can't do that as I'd have to return to England or go to Germany. Either way I'm done for."

"Your only other option is as I said before, is to marry a Swedish girl."

"I don't know, I like it here but I'm not really sure."

One day the Norwegian window cleaner and I were driven out to a factory where we were told to clean the windows. The problem was that as soon as I put the water on the windows it froze. I had no idea what to do and neither did the Norwegian, as he approached me with the same problem. I suggested that we go across the road to the cafe and have some breakfast. Shortly afterwards Bjorn arrived and he had a container of paraffin. He added this to the water and it never froze, and we finished cleaning the factory windows. Which believe me were very grubby.

Whilst I was in the factory a young man asked, "Why are you in Sweden?"

I replied, "For the midnight sun."

"No, you're here for the women." He said.

I didn't want to stay in Sweden for Christmas because they had fish for their main meal and I don't like fish. Also I'd read in one of the music papers that the Who would be performing Tommy at the London Coliseum. I wrote to my parents and told them I'd be home for Christmas and also asked them to get me a ticket to see the Who at the Coliseum and to buy a record for me called 'Birth' by The Peddlers. I bought a ticket for the boat for England and said to Bjorn, "I am leaving next week."

On my last day at the window cleaners Bjorn said to me. "My father is very sad to see you go."

"Thank you, maybe I get a work permit and come back." I replied.

"You can always work here."

"Thank you," I replied as we shook hands.

One of the last things I did in Sweden was to buy the album of Easy Rider. I'd looked for it everywhere, but eventually found it in an electrical shop by the harbour; I'd also bought Ogden's Nut Gone Flake by the Small Faces.

Peter drove me to the harbour and came with me to my cabin he shook hands with me and so it was that I left Sweden and set sail for Tilbury in Essex, which would be but a short train ride to London.

I discovered that I was in the same cabin as The Animals and asked, "Where's Eric Burdon?"

"He's left the band and is now in America."

They gave me lots of whiskey to drink and I was sick. The following morning when I joined the band for breakfast I was asked by one of the girls on the boat to sign her autograph book. Having signed her book one of the band said. "Every time, we get a new member."

Prior to disembarking everyone had to go through customs I was wearing my ski coat, which I had open revealing my yellow ice hockey sweater. I was called aside by the authorities who made notes and sent me on my way. I bid the band farewell and disembarked. Apparently at the time the Swedish were giving English visitors to Sweden a hard time. I can only assume that by entering Sweden first of all by train and then hitching I had avoided this close scrutiny. Perhaps the customs officials thought I was Swedish and hence they scrutinised me.

At the railway station I bought a single ticket for London and also a copy of Melody Maker. As I waited for the train, I was chatting to a guy when two men approached and one of them asked me.

"Is your name Bristow?"

"No. It's Bryson!"

Come with us you're a deserter from the Navy."

I handed my Melody Maker to the guy I'd been chatting to and accompanied the men to their car.

CHAPTER TWENTY FOUR

As I sat in the car I thought, *I won't be seeing the Who play Tommy at the Coliseum and also, my taste of freedom looks like it's finished.*

The detectives dropped me off at the local police station and placed me with my high pack in front of a portly uniformed sergeant and departed.

The sergeant took one look at my hair which hadn't been cut since August and said. "Skinheads are all the rage now." "What, those cunts!"

"Mind your language there are ladies present."

At this for some unknown reason I had visions of women who resembled the females of the Russian shot putting team. My thoughts were interrupted as the sergeant said, "The navy works a five day week now."

I stood there and said nothing whilst the sergeant took down my details speaking out loud. "Build slim, complexion fair. What colour are your eyes son?"

"Brown."

Having finished he locked me in a cell until two leading regulators from the navy arrived who deposited my 'luggage' and me and in the rear of a van. As we travelled off I felt like a lion that'd been caught, enclosed in a cage and lost all sense of freedom and soon my mane would be cut. As for the regulators they never said a word to me. It was as if I was just an insignificant package to be delivered.

We stopped en route and the regulators bought themselves some fish and chips and by the look of their bulging stomachs they didn't need to eat. I wanted to cry out, "Oi, what about me, I'm starving!" But I never did, to them I suppose I never existed.

Finally the van went under an archway in Kensington. The regulators unlocked me and said. "Pick up your kit and follow us."

We entered a large split-level building and stopped at the higher level where a lean looking Regulating Petty Officer (R.P.O.) took charge and said. "Put your pack on the table."

All three began to empty out the contents of my high pack and search it thoroughly.

"Oi! What do you think you're doing?" I asked. "The police never did anything like this."

The R.P.O. stared at me saying, "We, are more thorough than the police. You may be carrying drugs. So far, we've been lenient with you and we haven't locked you up. We'll be eating soon and we can let you watch the telly, but if you carry on like this we'll keep you locked up until the Portsmouth lot arrive."

I said nothing. One of the leading regulators handed over a letter to the R.P.O., who said, "Been writing to one of your hoppos have you? Get his name and we can punish him for withholding evidence."

What a fool I'd been for keeping a few letters. I later discovered my friend (Gary) underwent number nine punishment. This meant stoppage of leave and grog and extra work for a number of days.

Taking my time I begrudgingly repacked my things and was then escorted down to the lower part which was dominated by a long wooden table and a television. I ate in silence and watched an episode of Star Trek. It was something about a large cigar shaped object in space but unfortunately the leading regulators arrived from Portsmouth and to this day, I still don't know how that episode ended.

By now it was dark and I don't remember much of the drive to Portsmouth Barracks but what I do recall is as we drove under the archway which had inscribed on it H.M.S Victory, I thought sarcastically, *I bet Nelson would've been proud of me.*

Once again I was bundled out of the vehicle and told, "Remove your coat."

It was locked up in a cage, together with my high pack. I was given some bed linen and taken upstairs to my cell. We walked along a corridor with no windows and only doors along both sides. We stopped at a door and I was put inside the cell and locked up. There were bars up high, a wooden bench which doubled as my bed and the walls were made of bricks painted grey.

CHAPTER TWENTY FIVE

The following morning I was awoken early and escorted to the heads, to wash, shave and change into a set of number 8's (working clothes) and packed away my civvies.

Back in the cell the guard removed my breakfast dishes and offered me a selection of books. Oddly enough I chose one about Sweden. Reading it I yearned to be released and return to Sweden. I'm not sure if it was homesickness or just the thought of being caught and once again being back in the navy. After lunch, one of the guards unlocked my cell and said, "The Chief wants to see you."

I sat opposite the Chief, who was a large man, and as he offered me coffee said, "What have you been up to then? We had one rating who returned he was a bit like you, long hair and a bag over his shoulder and he said he'd burgled houses which, when we called the police, he denied."

I told him my story and when I got to the bit about staying with Peter and his wife he said.

"Did you fuck her?"

"No."

"You're not a sailor then."

I remained silent thinking it was obvious. After all, that's why I'd left because I didn't want to be a sailor.

When I ended my story he said, "In the morning the bosun will offer you a cup of coffee. Don't accept it as then it will make him feel uncomfortable."

The following morning having carried out my ablutions and had breakfast, I was shown into the bosun's office. Whilst being questioned the weekend duty chief put his head round the door and said, "I see you never took my advice and you've accepted the coffee. So, did you fuck that bloke's wife?"

"No."

"You're not a sailor."

He closed the door and left. I didn't understand his reason for wanting to upset the bosun; after all, the weekend chief had taken me into his confidence and asked me what I did whilst on the run.

The bosun who was a thin man said, "There's not much we can do until your docs arrive. What we will do is arrange an escort and get your picture taken, then you can have a haircut, after which you can go and buy some provisions for DQ's."

"But I haven't any money, only Swedish money."

"Don't worry about that. It'll all be taken care of."

Eventually my escort, which consisted of two gash hands, were told by the bosun's mate (a leading hand), "You two will accompany the prisoner all week, or until he goes to DQ's."

They were all right, as they weren't regulators and were interested in where I'd been and what I'd done. The youngest one was a slim cook and he said, "Where did you go to when you jumped ship?"

"Sweden."

"Wow! What was it like?"

"You'll have to excuse him, he's never been abroad," said the older, taller escort.

"But you're a cook. Surely you must have been abroad?"

"No. Nothing but land bases so far. So, what was Sweden like?"

"I got there at the end of August and practically every girl I saw was a gorgeous blonde?"

"Did you fuck any of them?" asked the older escort.

"One or two."

"How long were you in Sweden for?" The cook asked.

I told them about my exploits in Holland and Sweden and the older escort said, "Better than being in the navy then?"

"Well, for a short while it was. But it was getting cold in Holland so I decided to hitch back to Sweden and see if I could get political asylum."

"I take it you never got it," the cook said.

Eventually we arrived at the building where my photograph was to be taken, which I thought would be done by a naval photographer. Wrong! I was placed in a photo booth and so by way of rebellion, I turned my back to the screen. The older of the two escorts looked at the prints as they came out of the booth and said, "You pratt! I don't know what the chief'll say; we'll have to take them again. Which no doubt will be deducted from your pay."

"What pay?" I exclaimed.

The second time I opened up my eyes and it gave them an odd look.

We returned and the bosun looked at the photos saying. "Bit odd, but then the photo booth affects people in different ways. As for the first lot, you'll pay for that," he looked at the escort, "Right you two take him to get his haircut."

After which the bosun said, "Now you look more like a sailor."

My escort and the bosun's mate accompanied me to the shop where I purchased soap, razor blades, and shampoo. At first I only picked out carbolic soap, to wash my clothes with, but the bosun's mate who was paying for the items said, "You'll want other soap as well; otherwise you'll have skin like leather."

CHAPTER TWENTY SIX

My kit and documents arrived and I changed into my number 1 uniform. Luckily the only kit that was missing were my bed sheets. Having been issued with a cap tally of HMS Victory, I tied it on and smiled because it was as if Nelson was looking down at me with a somewhat jaundiced eye. Finally my escorts, together with all the other men were marched across the parade ground to the Commander's office. We stood outside until the Master at Arms beckoned us in and the R.P.O. cried out, "Prisoner and escort. Attention. Quick march, left wheel. Prisoner and escort, halt! Prisoner one pace forward march! Prisoner off cap! Prisoner and escort! Stand at ease . . . . Stand easy."

I stood in front of a dais, behind which stood a stout commander, who said, "Naval Airman Bryson. Do you plead guilty, or not guilty, to desertion?"

"Are you sure you have the right man in front of you?"

"What on earth are you on about? Do you plead guilty or not guilty, to desertion?"

"And I'll repeat, do you have the right man in front of you?"

"Believe me; I have the right man in front of me."

"But you said, Naval Airman Bryson and I, am Naval Air Mechanic Bryson?"

"Oh is that what you're wittering on about. Yes, I have the right man in front of me and do you plead guilty, or not guilty to desertion?"

"I'm not pleading to that. There's no such thing as desertion."

"I cannot believe what I'm hearing. Do you plead guilty or not guilty, to desertion?"

"I think you heard me all right. I said there's no such thing as desertion, so I didn't plead."

"I hope you're not just going to stand there and make a mockery of these proceedings?"

"No, that's not my intention."

"Good, perhaps we can get on now. Do you plead guilty, or not guilty to desertion?"

"I'm not pleading to that, as there's no such thing as desertion."

"What on earth are you gibbering on about? I merely asked you a question to which normally, I receive a reply from. But oh no, not you, you try and make a farce out of these proceedings. So I'll ask you one more time. Do you plead guilty, or not guilty, to desertion?"

"And I'll repeat, there's no such thing as desertion."

"What do you mean, there's no such thing as desertion?"

"Like I said, there's no such thing as desertion, because, it wouldn't stand up in a civil law court."

"You are brought here on a charge of desertion and all you've done so far is to gibber on and avoid answering me. Now you bring up an issue of civil law. So I'll ask you one more time. Do you plead guilty, or not guilty, to desertion?"

"If all you're going to do is repeat yourself, then I'll plead not guilty."

"Did you intend to return to your ship?"

"I don't think so."

"I'll take that as an obstinate no then."

"You can take it for what you like, but I may well have returned to my ship, I can't really say for sure. I might have got bored and decided to return to my ship." I flippantly replied.

"You cannot just come and go as you please. This is the Royal Navy, not, a part time job. When you joined the Navy, you agreed to abide by naval law, which governs everything you, or I do. The Navy does not employ drifters, who just turn up for work, as and when they please. So did you intend to return to your ship?"

"First you ask me if I deserted and now you're asking me if I intended to return to my ship. You ought to make up your mind as to which question you want me to answer?"

"I want you to answer both questions."

"Let me see if I can get this into some sort of perspective. First of all, you want me to give an answer to a fictitious charge and then you ask me if I intended to return to my ship. Is that correct?"

"At last, the message seems to be getting through to you. You said you plead not guilty to desertion."

"That's right. So you were listening then. I'd like it noted that although I pleaded not guilty, I'm pleading to a fictitious charge."

"So you're back to that again. Don't try and get funny with me now. Did you intend to return to your ship? I will not accept any perverse answers from you, all I want is a simple yes or no, and don't go off at a tangent about civil law. As I've already said you, are governed by the same law as me, and that, is naval law."

"Well if you put it like that, I don't suppose I would've returned to my ship."

"By your own words then, you're guilty."

"Oh that's good. I thought the law stated everyone was innocent until proved guilty. I suppose that excludes the navy does it? Because I said I pleaded not guilty to desertion, and yet you say I'm guilty.

"I shall ignore your comments. Is there anything else?"

"Yes there is!"

"Do you want to tell me? If you do, you'll also have to tell the Commodore."

"Well I'm certainly not going to waste my breath on you and the Commodore, so I'll tell the Commodore."

"Stood over for Commodore's."

The R.P.O. then burst into animation. "Prisoner and escort! Attention. Prisoner! On cap. Prisoner and escort, about turn. Prisoner, one pace forward march. Prisoner and escort! Quick march, right wheel."

When we were once again walking across the parade ground both of the escorts said, "You were hilarious. The state of the commander, he was about to blow a fuse."

"It doesn't matter, I'm done for anyway."

"But aren't you scared?" asked the cook.

"What of?"

"Going into D.Q.'s."

"The scariest bit is over. I'm back in the Navy aren't I?"

"But you'll be locked up and it's an awful place." The other escort said. "OK, so it's a deterrent, but for me, it all ended when I was picked up by the police at Tilbury. If I had the chance. Oh I don't know I wished I'd stayed in Sweden. I was earning good money, the flat I stayed in was nice and you know why I came back?"

"No," they replied.

"Because the Swedish have fish for Christmas Dinner. Goodness only knows what I'll have for Christmas dinner now."

"I don't think you'll have to worry about Christmas dinner," replied the older escort.

CHAPTER TWENTY SEVEN

There was some hold up so I couldn't see the Commodore until two days later. Once again I was stood in front of the dais, behind which stood this decrepit looking old man. I would add here, the rank of commodore is virtually redundant as most officers tend to go from the command of something like an aircraft carrier, where they hold the rank of Captain, to Admiral. So where they dug this decrepit old relic up from goodness only knows. Once again I was stood easy, with my cap in my hand and the questioning began.

"Naval Airman Bryson, do you plead guilty, or not guilty to desertion."

"As I told the Commander, I am a naval air mechanic, not a naval airman. And, I plead not guilty."

"Did you intend to return to your ship?"

"No."

"Therefore I find you guilty."

"But there's no such thing as desertion."

"I am not going to be put through the same rigmarole as the Commander. I believe there are mitigating circumstances."

"That's right."

"What are they?"

"Your advert's a lie!"

"What do you mean?"

"Well, your advert clearly states I can further my education."

"That's perfectly correct."

"Oh no it's not."

"Explain yourself."

"Well there I was working on the helicopter and I used to get time off to study for my G.C.E.'s. But one day, I was told instead of going to my lessons, I had to work on the helicopter."

"There's a perfectly good correspondence course. Is there anything else?"

"Yes. The conditions of work."

"We've all been through it."

"Oh, it's all right for you, with a steward attending to your every needs. But you try working in a hangar in the winter with the doors open. It's no joke, I can tell you."

"You, think the navy owes you a living!"

I was going to say, no, but I remained silent. I could see the silly old sod was getting angry and I thought I'd said enough.

Then it was back to the cells and both my escorts said, "You weren't as funny as you were last time. It's as if you don't care." The older escort replied.

"Well, I don't. I told 'im what I thought. It's up to 'im now. Anyway, he looked as if he was well past retirement age. Where'd they dig 'im up from?"

Just before they left me the cook said, "I'd like to travel."

"That's why I joined the navy in the first place," I replied, "To travel, but if you really want to go to sea put in for a ship or swap drafts with another cook."

"Thanks, I'll do that."

"Don't blame me if you don't like it at sea, but all being well, you should at least go abroad and try and go on a small ship, not an aircraft carrier."

"Thanks, good luck." Both escorts said.

I bid them both farewell and on Friday afternoon all of us prisoners were lined up to hear our sentences. Most of them got twenty-eight days, but when the bosun called out my name, he called out. "Forty-two days."

Afterwards, the bosun's mate came over to me and said. "Have you been in before?"

"No."

"Well, you must have upset the commodore or something, because for a first offence you normally only get twenty-eight days." He then stood to one side and addressed us all, "Now pay attention to the bosun."

"Tomorrow morning you'll all be dispatched to Detention Quarters. I don't care what you did to get into this predicament, but whatever you do in D.Q.'s, keep your nose clean. Don't, under any circumstances, play them up. Just do your time, get your maximum remission and come out. Dismiss."

That night, prior to going to sleep I thought about the Commander and the Commodore and what they'd say about me. I could see them in the wardroom.

"Well, how did you get on with that naval airman." asked the Commander.

"You were right. What an impudent young pup! Furthermore, he never once acknowledged my rank by calling me sir." replied the Commodore.

"I knew you'd have trouble with him. Incidentally, what were his mitigating circumstances?"

"Something about our advert being a lie and he was unable to continue his studies. Then, to add insult to injury, he started on about the conditions

of work. God knows, we've all been through it. Sounds as if they're recruiting a right load of namby pamby mother's boys."

"Quite right. So, what sentence did you give him?"

"I'd have sentenced him to sixty, or even ninety days. That would've really shown him. Still, as a first time offender, I gave him the maximum I could and that, was 42 days."

"Quite right too that'll teach the impudent dog a lesson."

"I'd like to have seen his face when he heard his sentence." The commodore replied.

"I've no doubt you wiped the grin from his impudent face. Another pink gin? This one's on me and we'll raise our glasses in a toast. To stamp out impudence on the lower decks."

CHAPTER TWENTY EIGHT

Having washed shaved and eaten breakfast, I dressed in my Number 8s and assembled outside the cells with the other prisoners.

It was a dark and cold Saturday morning in December as I loaded my kitbag along with my high pack into the truck, which was waiting outside the cells. Together with the other prisoners; I climbed aboard the truck and sat on a wooden bench waiting to be chauffeur driven to Royal Navy Detention Quarters, just down the road from R.N. Barracks, otherwise known as, H.M.S. Victory.

It was still dark as we entered DQs and were marched into an office where our belongings were checked and stored until we left. Everyone I saw who was in charge, was a Chief GI, except that is, for the Chief Cook and Master at Arms. As we signed for our belongings the Chief looked at my Swedish money and said. "What's this, Monopoly Money?"

"Excuse me, but its Swedish Krona and worth about eighty pounds."

"Very good. Just sign for it. You can have it upon your release."

Prior to being marched over to the cellblock we were told. "You call everyone in here, Sir and you will be given a class number, which in effect means which week of the year, you arrived in this establishment. So all of you will be in 51 class. You will all be issued with a band to slip over your belt and you will also notice that there is a 53 class, who wear green bands. That's because they're green cunts, who were here previously in the last two years."

From the office we were marched to the cellblock. As we entered I looked up through the wire netting above us and saw another two floors of cells.

The Chief who was in charge of us, looked aloft to another chief, who was standing on the first floor and said. "Chief Petty Officer Bates, Sir."

"Yes sir."

"New intake Sir."

"Thank you Sir. I'll be down in a moment."

Oh my God! I thought, *what on earth is this place? They even call each other, Sir.*

We were marched along to the shaving locker where our razors would be kept for the duration of our stay. The other chief walked down the stairs, which the navy referred to as a ladder and joined us by the shaving locker and explained about shaving routine.

"First thing in the morning your room will be unlocked. By this time you will be dressed in your 8s, which will be the standard dress during your stay here. You will be told to stand by your doors with your drinking mugs, from where you will be ordered to collect your razor which will be placed in this locker." The chief pointed to a black metal locker behind him. "Your razor will be in the pigeon hole that is the same number as your room. You will also collect in your shaving mug, hot water to shave with. You then return to your room and shave, with your door open." He paused, "You do not shave from your drinking mug!"

He then looked at the other chief and said, "All yours sir. Show them how to clean their rooms and to which room they've been allocated."

"Aye aye sir."

Then, we were marched over to a 'room', it was narrow and on one side was a wooden bed upon which was placed a mattress and bed linen. The bed had to be made up as laid down in standing orders. This meant that it was made with a counterpane on top of the blankets and sheets; the top sheet was turned down to expose the pillow. On the opposite side was a wooden table underneath which was placed a wooden stool. Upon the table there was a plastic mug, a shaving brush, soap, toothbrush, toothpaste a bible and a book. Up high was a barred window, underneath it was an oblong piece of shiny metal, in the corner a plastic bowl and a shiny galvanized bucket.

We gathered around as the chief said. "This is what your room will be like. The bucket, which you can see at the far end of your room, is in case you get caught short in the night. The plastic bowl, is for washing in and the mug contains drinking water and also, after unlock, and as you've just been told, you will be drilled down to the shaving locker carrying your mug empty."

The chief went into the 'room' and pulled out a polished piece of metal and said. "This will serve as your shaving mirror. Also, you will be allowed to write one letter a week. As for smokers, you will be allowed a cigarette a day. After you've eaten your midday meal you will be engaged in plaiting rope, which goes to make mats. You will be instructed about this on Monday. If any of you are caught lying on your bed, you will be placed before the Commander." He then lifted up the stool and turned it over saying, "Also you will have to clean the woodwork and tin gear." He then pointed to the bucket, mirror, table and chair. "Mind you, for the first week, you will not mix with the others nor will you be allowed to have any cigarettes. The only time you will be allowed to speak, is in the classroom. At all other times you will say nothing. In the second week, you will be allowed to have your midday meal with the others and you may speak to them. Do you understand?"

"Yes sir." We mumbled.

"What was that you said?"

"Yes sir." We repeated, only this time it was louder.

I looked at the woodwork in the cell; it was white whereas the tin gear was gleaming. In fact I could've used the bucket as a mirror. We were then marched over to the mat room, where we were shown how to plait the hemp. We were all issued with a quantity of it marched to our 'rooms' and locked in.

My 'room' was located on the first floor at the far end of the cellblock above the television and I sat on my stool thinking to myself. *If this is my room, then where's my key. As for the staff, it was as if I'd arrived at the retirement home, for old GIs.* I looked up to the barred window, which was open and was too high for me to close. The heating was supplied by a pipe, which ran along the bottom of the 'room', below the window.

I then started to plait the hemp. It was really course but I soon got into a rhythm of plaiting the stuff. Also not being too sure about what I could, or couldn't do, I began reading the bible that only contained The New Testament, which during my stay in DQs I actually read all the way through. Whether this made me more religious or not, I cannot say. I was still a lapsed Catholic and as far as I could make out, there were some good stories in the bible. This solitude drove a lot of men out of their minds, as for me I'd spent so long alone, that it didn't really affect me. Firstly whilst on HMS Eagle all I'd done was sit in the Burma row waiting for the helicopter to land and during that time, I read many books. Also I'd spent time alone as I'd hitched from Sweden to Holland and back to Sweden. The answer to avoid boredom is to keep your mind active, hence we were all given a hunk of hemp to plait and that's why I read the New Testament. I suppose you have to learn to live with yourself, but also all the time alone gave me time to think. I wanted to break out of the place and if necessary go back to Sweden and never return to England. For me, DQs just made me hate the navy even more.

The only method I had of determining when it was the end of the day was when the light in my cell was turned out. I had no watch and could only guess what the time was and as for when I got up or went to bed, I really have no idea about as I hadn't noticed any clocks around the place.

The following morning I could hear in the distance a hammering on the doors and gradually it got closer. Until the hammering was on my door and my light came on. I got up and dressed.

Next I heard the order, "Unlock!" Shouted out.

Gradually every cell door was opened and I noticed that my breakfast was placed outside my door. I took it in and ate it. After a while the next orders were bellowed out from below.

"Up behind your doors, with your drinking mug."

I had to retrieve mine from the table and quickly stood in the doorway, waiting for the next order.

"Standby. Out!"

At this command every prisoner came out of their cells and stood staring in front of them. As for me, I wanted to look at the others and I thought about what I'd been taught in school when playing basketball. This was, that although you look ahead, you could also look either side of you. This I did, keeping my head straight and just looking either side of me with my eyes. Then the Chief GI started again.

"When you come down to the shaving locker, collect your razor from the pigeon hole with your room number on it. Collect your hot water, in your drinking mug. Return to your room and shave. When you shave, keep your door open and do not shave from your drinking mug! You then wash your razor and return it to the locker, open. Then carry out, slop out routine." There was a short pause. "Towards the centre ladder. Right and left, turn. Double march!"

I returned to my cell and shaved, from my drinking mug. This was not in disobedience to the orders. There was no way I wanted to stay longer in that place than I had to. It was just that I hadn't been listening properly, I would add here, that in that respect nothing has changed, as I'm still not a very good listener, well so I've been told, more of a raconteur. Fortunately, I did not have a very strong beard growth. That was my early morning routine for my entire stay in DQs. Although Sunday was the exception as we had breakfast served in our 'rooms'. Normally we shaved and then went down to the galley, for our breakfast. I must add that after a while, I did pour the hot water into the bowl and use it the proper way.

That Sunday and every consecutive one I went to church, as the only alternative was to remain locked up all day, going to church relieved the boredom of Sunday in DQs.

Church was merely a room set aside in DQs for worship.

On Monday the day began in the manner I've already described and once we'd completed shaving and slop out, we had to assemble outside on the parade ground, where we fell in by classes and had to number.

The Chief G.I then bellowed out. "Right turn. Double march." We ran around the parade ground and over a small assault course.

Up until this time I felt really fit, after all, I'd been carrying my pack around Europe, but after going over the assault course, I felt totally knackered.

I looked behind me at the assault course as one of the GIs went over it and was spurred on by the other chiefs who cried out. "Go on Bomber!" I have no idea how old the man was, but I thought he was very fit. He was probably a lot fitter than men half his age.

We then went into the galley to collect our breakfast after which we returned to our rooms. Once again we were locked in, then we were unlocked again, returned our plates to the galley and then it was toilet routine.

This was a complete farce. We all lined up to use the toilets. We were not allowed to speak to each other and it was more or less, shitting by numbers. Once, when I was waiting my turn the Chief banged on someone's door and cried out.

"Come on now! You've had enough time to give berth!"

Later on, another prisoner said to me as we queued up for the loo. "I heard about this man who had his toilet built by a stream and he used to sit there for as long as he liked, fishing."

"I know what you mean. This shitting by numbers is awful. When I get out, I'm never going to rush the time I spend in the bog." "Me too. A shit should be savoured," he replied.

We then went about our various tasks. For my first class, it began by reporting to the Chief who was in charge of the hemp and we were all given a diabolical haircut. Mind you the Chief did say as he cut our hair, or rather shaved our heads. Well, not all of our heads, only the bit that was below our caps.

"I can understand why you lot desert. In my day we didn't spend so long at sea and there seemed to be more places for us to call into."

We were then drilled back into the main block to have a wash. Once a week we carried out dhobi sessions, where we showered and washed our kit. After that, we had lectures about what, I can't for the life of me remember.

One of the first lessons we had was PT. The PTI was an amazing man and he was certainly not what you'd expect of a PTI. They were usually very fit, whereas this one was rather rotund. He had a shock of white hair, a white pullover, white shorts and white socks and plimsoles. He spoke in a deep gruff voice and said. "Lie down!"

A rest at last, I thought. How wrong I was.

"Now raise your legs about six inches off the deck," the PTI growled. "Now part your legs. Hold it! Don't let them drop. Legs together. Who said you could lower your legs?" Throughout this torturous exercise, farts rang out across the room. Having done a few exercises, the PTI asked us what we'd done to be in DQs. I can't remember what one bloke said, but the PTI replied with,

"You think the navy owes you a living." As the Commander had said that to me, perhaps that was the standard comment of old salts.

We were also drilled on the parade ground and one of the GIs was gaunt and didn't so much give out orders as scream the orders rather manically, and so he'd been named by someone as, 'The Screaming Skull.'

The first week was hell for me as the only time I could speak was in the classroom and then it was only to the Chief, or sometimes we had a marine instructing us. The first time I could actually speak to my fellow inmates was Monday week at lunch. The only time we were allowed to speak was at lunch and dinner, when we sat at tables to eat. I actually met the sailor who'd fallen overboard on H.M.S Eagle. He'd been drunk and not as was rumoured on Brasso, but beer. In the evening we were allowed to watch the television, which consisted of Hector's House, followed by the news and then confinement to our 'room'. After lunch, we were once again locked in our rooms. Occasionally I'd hear one of the Chiefs banging on somebody's door. They were no doubt committing the sin of doing nothing, except lying on their bed.

I was scared, so I either plaited the hemp or read. I knew when I was being watched, as I could hear the cover of the 'spy' hole being pushed to one side, to allow the duty chief to ensure that us prisoners were working or at least, not lying on our beds. I wonder what would have happened if I'd blocked the 'spy' hole up in some way or another?

Apart from the bible the other book we had, had a few bits by Baden Powell about looking after yourself. There were odd quotes like. "A gentleman is a bloke what cleans his toes."

One of the guys I met had also been on the run, but he'd got a job at Middle Earth in London and said, "It was amazing when King Crimson came on and did 'The Court of the Crimson King.' When they started to play, the whole place was silent and then when it became louder. It was just brilliant."

Probably the worse day for me in DQs was Christmas Day. It was the worst one of my life. We were paraded outside and one rating received a Christmas card to which the Chief GI remarked, "And don't let it happen again, next year."

Those of us that were going to a church service went, after which, we were kept locked up all day. We had a Christmas dinner, but otherwise it was rather miserable. Having eaten my Christmas meal I could hear from the television below me on the ground floor, what sounded like the film, 'A White Christmas'. For me it was a dank, dark, grey Christmas.

New Years Eve was worse. I lay in my bed; I never slept that well, still don't, I think I'm a bit of an insomnomaniac. All of a sudden I heard ships horns blasting out through the dark night; it's probably the navy's way of welcoming in the New Year. I suppose if anyone had been asleep in DQs they'd certainly have been woken up by that cacophony.

I gained my full remission and was released after 28 days, I suppose in hindsight I'm glad about having a laugh with the Commander and Commodore, after all, I'd only served four days more than I would've done if I'd kept my mouth shut. I felt really fit and was sent to H.M.S Daedalus, which is the main base for the Fleet Air Arm. That first week, I was once again misemployed and just did odd jobs about the base; I even arranged to get a lift home for the weekend. This was not to be as one day I was called into the office and told.

"Your draft's come through. You're being sent to H.M.S. Eagle. I have no more details but when I hear, I'll let you know."

I thought to myself, *'I wonder what they'll do with me? Probably back to being misemployed.'*

A day or so later I was once again called into the office where I was duly informed, "You're being drafted to the S.A.R. on board the Eagle."

CHAPTER TWENTY NINE

I dismally returned to the Eagle and was once again in my old mess.

Pete said, "Where'd you go to?"

"Sweden and Holland."

"Oh we thought you'd gone to India."

"No, I went for political asylum and then I hitched down to Holland."

"Your kit was sold."

"So what have I got left?"

My kitbag was handed to me and all was well as only my sheets had been sold. So to compensate I slept in the mattress cover. It was like sleeping in a thin sleeping bag.

"I thought you'd gone back to America." Davy said.

"Yeah, I would've liked to if only to see Woodstock."

On Friday I said to Paddy and John, the flight chiefs, "I'm going on weekend leave."

I thought that they would try and stop me, because I certainly didn't intend coming back. Instead, they said nothing; perhaps they thought I was too much of a problem.

So I grabbed my watch card and said to my messmates. "I'm not coming back, so I'm going to try and fake it and not put my card in for leave. If it should go wrong, could one of you grab my card please?"

They said they'd do it for me. But I didn't need them as I never put my card in just made the gesture.

I got home to see my parents and my dad said, "It's good to see you back home again son."

Mum said, "We had a surprise over Christmas, Peter visited us." He was the guy I'd stayed with in Sweden.

After a while I said, "I'm not going back."

Mum said, "It's the wrong time of the year. It's too cold. Anyway, your father is going to work on something for you. Remember when you had that crash on your scooter?"

"Yes."

"Well, your father's going to say it sent you a bit mad."

As we went along to the pub for Sunday lunch Mum said, "I remember when you'd not long deserted, your father and I were walking along this path, when we saw a naval van going along the road and I wondered if they were looking for you. I later discovered they were and the young sailor with the older ones wished that he could desert."

I returned to my ship where I was told that I had to see Lieutenant Stanton. I went into his cabin, he said, "Sit down. This afternoon we have to see the captain. Everyone who's been to DQs has to see him. So what are you going to say to him?"

"I'll just tell the captain."

"But don't you want to tell me first?"

"Not really." I felt sorry for Dave as he was a good bloke.

I got changed in to my No 1 uniform and went with Dave (Lt Stanton) to see the captain, who said. "Have you learned anything from your stay in DQs?"

"I don't think so; I still don't like the navy."

"What are your intentions now?"

"To be honest, I think I'll desert again."

"Let us suppose that everyone who wanted to leave, took that attitude. Where would we be? After a while some of them would drift back and so, we can't take that chance on how many would return. We just can't have this sort of thing. There are far more deserving cases than you on board who wish to leave. I will say that you're a pain in the rear, but I won't bend over to get you out."

Later on in the mess, Dodger (one of the aircrew) said, "How you'd get on with the captain?"

"I told him I'd desert again."

"I wouldn't have you on my ship. I'd throw you off now, you're a liability."

Shortly after that, we changed pilots and some of the mechanics and electricians. Our new man in charge was Lt B.P. Davies. He was a right stuck up person and I asked the aircrew to find out what B.P. stood for. At the time there was a band called the Spencer Davis Band, they made such tunes as 'Somebody Help Me', which I used to go around singing. I also discovered we'd lost a petty officer. He'd got fed up and had also gone to DQs, but unlike me, he wasn't sent back to HMS Eagle. We also gained a doddery old petty officer. He was a three-badge man, (been in the navy for twelve years) but as far as I could ascertain, HMS Eagle was his first ship! Once we were at sea and this PO had seen me work he said to Pete, "You know, Bryson could be a very good mechanic."

To which Pete replied, "Smiler is a good mechanic!"

The ship set sail and when we had to spread the blades of the helicopter I was on the pole, on my own. This meant I had to clamp the pole over the end of the blade and hoist it up into the air, whilst Pete hammered in the pin. It went fine unless I didn't quite line up the pin and had to jiggle the blade around. Normally, this was a two man job, but I suppose as I'd just come from DQ's it was assumed that I would be fit enough to carry it out on my own. We then lashed down the helicopter and went along to the galley for breakfast and after which for me, it was back in the Burma Row. This is the passageway that runs alongside the chimney on the ship and it's always warm there, hence the title of Burma Row. It was back to reading books and waiting for the helicopter to land, when I merely had to refuel it, get a signature from the pilot and return to the Burma Row.

I heard later that the petty officer that got sent to DQs was quite funny. You see the lashings we used to tie down the helicopter were usually stowed in a gully that ran along the side of ship just below the flight deck. Sometimes when he was asked where to put the lashings he would reply with *"Throw them over the side."* No wonder he got sent to DQs. What happened to him, I have no idea about.

Most of the time at sea it wasn't rough but this may have been because the ship was so large. I can recall one occasion when flying was cancelled because the sea was rough and we were also being refuelled at sea.

It was in weather like this that Ed James asked me to give him a hand to collect the victuals for the coffee boat. He asked me as I was one of the few who weren't working and also wasn't lying in bed feeling sea sick. As we went aloft to the weather deck I could not believe what I saw. The sea was so rough that the RFA refuelling us was up and down in the sea like a bucking bronco and its stern screws, every now and again rose out of the sea. We then went higher up in the ship, I certainly felt queasy, but never threw up.

Also I took over the coffee boat. In the mess we had victuals that enabled us to have tea or coffee all the time and whoever ran it before wasn't very good and so I took over. All it entailed was collecting money from my messmates and going to collect the victuals and then everyone just helped themselves any time to tea and coffee, but once again it went wrong. You see running a coffee boat is supposed to be a profit making business. So I confronted my messmates who were moaning about the dysfunctional coffee boat.

I replied by saying, "Fine if you want this coffee boat to run for 24 hrs, then I will have to charge you more." They all agreed and this time it all went well, as for profit, I don't think I made that much, but we did have some of the pilots down to have a chat and I said to one of them.

"If I get hold of an officer's uniform, will you buy me a pint in the wardroom?"

To which he replied, "Smiler if you can get hold of an officer's uniform, I'll buy it off you." I only wanted a pint of beer, which apparently in the wardroom was very cheap.

The first port of call was Gibraltar, oh boy what a lark that was. The first shift to go ashore got into trouble. I think they returned drunk and someone lost one of his badges. As for me, I was part of the second wave to go ashore and I didn't think much of Gibraltar, it just seemed to be a long street with bars, so we had a few drinks and went back on board.

CHAPTER THIRTY

Then we stopped in France. Pete returned and couldn't speak. He'd been in a fight and some Frenchman had hit him and his tooth had gone through his tongue and he was on doctor's orders not to speak. We took bets on how long he could remain silent for. Needless to say it didn't last long. When I went ashore in France I went with Dan (he was new) and we entered a bar where he ordered pastis, whatever that is. It turned out to be Pernod or something like aniseed. Feeling hungry we decided to get something to eat so we chose a Chinese restaurant well we thought they'd speak English. Wrong!

I have no idea what we ordered but we got this soup that looked like snot with long bogeys in. Neither of us could eat it and so we left. I really don't know if we paid but then, I don't remember any Chinese chasing after us.

Our new pilot BP Davies organised what is termed as a run ashore. Which meant we went as a group, also I'd discovered what BP stood for. So the whole of the Eagle SAR was in some French bar and Lt Davies was talking to Al Hart, referring to him as Hart. So I butted in with, "Look we're ashore now, so you can call him Al. Tell you what, I'll call you by your first name and you, can call me Smiler."

"But you don't know my first name," he haughtily replied.

"Okay Bradley, or would you rather be called Brad? You can call me, Smiler!"

His initials stood for, Bradley Peregrine, but after that trip to a bar in France, I don't think we really got on. As far as I was concerned Dave was much better.

So my first trip to France was not a very good one and I was glad when we left and set sail for England. On the way it was my birthday. I had a magic tot glass as it never emptied the lads had also saved some beer for me, but I was too drunk to drink it. Also over the ship's radio the DJ played bands like Led Zeppelin and I was crying out. "I love you Robert!"

This was a reference to Robert Plant the lead singer of Led Zeppelin, but someone ran out of the mess, thinking that I was referring to him!

I was also writing to Agnetha the girl in Sweden and in my drunk state I said that I loved Agnetha, but when my mess mates found out who she was, they thought that I was off my rocker.

We were nearing Portsmouth when I was told to report to the sick bay where I saw the officer in charge. I went into his office and he said, "Be seated. You will be sent ashore at Portsmouth to see the shrink. Apparently your father thinks you're mad. Personally I can't see it myself. So why would he say you're mad?"

"I crashed when I was about sixteen, I was driving a scooter and I wasn't wearing a helmet. So it may have sent me mad." "Oh really, well it'll be up to the shrink to decide."

"When will I see him?"

"You will be informed when you are to see the shrink and you will wear number 1s. Do you understand?"

"Yes sir." I dismally replied.

"Dismiss."

So I duly went to see the shrink at HMS Victory (Portsmouth Barracks) and lo and behold, I bumped into an old school mate of mine, Geoff Cornish.

"Hello Geoff, how are you?"

"Hello Smiler, how're you doing?"

"I don't like the navy, I've deserted, I went to Sweden and Holland, but when I came back, I was sent to DQs." I laughed, "Actually, I talked my way out of 28 days into 42 days."

"You must be insane, same old Smiler. As for me I rather like it, I don't think I could go to DQs, the only thing is, I wished I'd joined the merchant navy and in that way, I'd be an officer."

"Yeah Mel (another old schoolmate) told me that. I'm off to see the shrink."

"What for?"

"To try and prove that I'm mad and get thrown out that way." "But it's really good, you get to travel."

"Are that's the problem, see I'm on aircraft carrier, I went to the States last summer, came back and deserted and I realised then that I should've just hitched around. It's a brilliant life. Work a bit, travel on and follow the sun. I suppose I've chosen the wrong path. I should've become a hippy and hitched around."

"A bit like a gypsy."

"I suppose so. By the way, did you take Diane's diary at school?" Geoff laughed and then told me that he'd shagged most of the good-looking girls in school. Well he was better looking than me and obviously, not so shy. Lucky bleeder! After a while we went our separate ways and as for the shrink, I really can't remember much about it. So it was back to sea and wait for the results.

Next port of call was Liverpool where we had to go ashore in uniform. I just wanted to get back home to London and the navy had put on a special train for sailors. The rail staff told every sailor, to catch the special train that had been laid on. I changed in the station loo into civvies and caught another faster train.

That weekend I went to a university to see a band and on the way back I met Ricky and Dodger on the train. They told me how people had changed into civvies and got on the naval train and been told off by the Naval Patrol. I was so glad I'd avoided that train.

Also I had to go back and see the doctor on board HMS Eagle, I once again sat in his room and he said, "I have the results of your test here and, it would prove that far from being insane, you are rather intelligent. Now as this test was carried out by the insistence of your father, if I were your father, I would tell you to get a job that you can't get out of."

"But I have one of those and quite frankly, I don't think much of it."

"Very good, I shall make a note of that. Return to your section."

Later that day I was in the mess and everyone was getting ready to go ashore in Liverpool, rumour had it that those that had stayed in Liverpool had no problem pulling girls as they seemed to like sailors. One of the bearded blokes from the helicopter squadron turned up in our mess. Looked at me and said, "Bryson, get your kit on, you're coming ashore with us!"

"So I put on my number one's and went ashore with Dodger, Ricky, LAM Johnson and the bearded bloke from the helicopter squadron, whose name, for the life of me, I cannot remember. It was a right laugh, plus I had never drunk so much in my life. We started at lunch and drank until closing time and then we wandered round the shops. Some time during the afternoon I threw up. Well at least it made room for the evening drinking session. I think in the end throughout the whole day I drank about 20 pints. I believe by going to DQs I had raised my status and as for the drinking, my status went up even higher. Eventually the ship left Liverpool and I knew that we were headed for Plymouth where we were to disembark for the final time.

Somewhere on the trip we went to Elgin in Scotland. I met a bloke whilst ashore, who was working with the Gannet's and I said, "Any chance I could have a flight in a Gannet? I really fancy being launched off the catapult."

"There may be a chance of you going off in the Gannet that collects the mail, but I don't think you'll have much luck. I'll find out for you." He replied.

"Thanks mate, if it comes off, I'll sort a flight for you in a helicopter."

Needless to say there wasn't much to do in Elgin. The Eagle was anchored off the coast, the weather was rough and we had to stay overnight at Lossiemouth, which then had Buccaneers.

I awoke in the lower bunk of a mess and looked up to a bunk opposite me and as I did, some bloke farted and his white underpants had a brown stain upon them. He just cried out, "Where's my wife!"

Also whilst at sea we underwent a situation as if we were at war and I arrived down in my mess to find it in total darkness. I asked what had happened and someone replied.

"Apparently we've been hit and this part of the ship is damaged. I was supposed to report to the sick bay with a broken leg. I told them to fuck off and go and play silly sailors elsewhere."

There appeared to be little else to do so I thought I'd go to bed. Eventually we all arrived back at HMS Seahawk (Culdrose) in Cornwall and even though we were still part of the Eagle SAR we knew we would soon be going our different ways. Hence we were all asked to put in a preference to where we wanted to go.

My first choice was for the PTA at Portland. This is a small section that has model aeroplanes, which are used for target practise, but they are not supposed to be hit. I think it's for the gunners and basically the members of the PTA get flown around the world with their model planes. Having filled out my form I had to go and see Brad, who looked at my form and said, "Why do you think you will get on the PTA?"

"Ah well, you have to live out of a suitcase which is not everyone's cup of tea. But as I'm not married or engaged, I think the life would suit me."

"I don't think there's much chance of you getting on to the PTA section and what's this HMS Chrysanthemum?"

"I heard that they needed an aircraft mechanic on board." *Actually I had no idea about that at all, as it's a ship that's moored in the Thames and I thought I'd be able to live at home and commute into town.*

"I see, well I don't hold out much chance of that either, I'll see if we can get you to Portland."

"OK." I reluctantly replied.

We chatted about my general work and behaviour, after which Brad said, "You've sat here talking to me and yet, you haven't once called me sir."

"Is that it then, have you finished with me?"

"Yes I have, you insubordinate person."

There was another day when Brad had turned up in an old A55 pickup he owned. Apparently he had a smallholding. Seeing this van outside the window I said to him, "Excuse me sir, but is that your van outside?"

"Yes it is why?"

"Tell you what, I'll do you a favour. I'll risk being seen off and give you a fiver for it."

"Get out of here and go and do some work. I've just spent more than that on tyres!" Brad replied.

I thought that life at Cornwall would be back to normal, but even here I was wrong. Stan now had a girlfriend and Tony was married. So I used to go for drinks with Ellis, I remember walking along the road with him singing, *Twenty first Century Schizoid Man*. It was a song by King Crimson. Also I'd chatted up a girl in Falmouth and was due to see her of an evening, but a message came over the tannoy system for me to report to the gatehouse where the Chief of the Watch said, "Got a message here from some girl, she can't make it tonight."

"Thanks chief," I replied as I dismally returned to my mess, plus I had no way of contacting her as I never had her phone number.

Another time I was walking along Helston when someone shouted out, "Bryson!"

"Hello Tommy," I replied, he'd been one of the first aircrew. "I've heard good reports of you."

"Thanks Tommy, see you later." With that I wandered to the pub, which is no doubt what the good report was that Tommy had heard of.

Word of my drinking binge in Liverpool had obviously got round. One day Dan said to me, "I'm going for a late tot, my mate's in charge of the rum."

Late tot was doled out to those that missed the lunchtime tot and it was virtually neat, very tasty. I later discovered that the PO in charge was Jimmy Rowan, whom I'm pretty sure was the same Jimmy Rowan, along with Jake Fordham, that had voted me the ugliest bloke of the year. But I never went to late tot to find out. As for Jake, I once got a lift home with him to London, he'd also been promoted to the rank of a petty officer. Another time I hitched to London I got a lift in the Admiral's car, or someone high up in the navy.

I was still very disenchanted with life in the navy, but that summer there was to be a music festival at Bath featuring Led Zeppelin and so I bought a ticket for it.

CHAPTER THIRTY ONE

But I really was fed up with the navy. The job on the PTA didn't look like it would materialise but I'd also taken an exam to see if I was good enough to be trained as a leading hand, which if I had passed, would hopefully mean I would be sent on the leading hands course. Passing that with a high enough mark, even with my past could result in being asked if I wanted to stay at school and train for a petty officer.

It was not to be and I decided to end my life in the navy once and for all, but how should I do it? Then it occurred to me why not wreck a helicopter? So the following day one of the helicopters was out ready to fly whilst the other was in the hangar. I went into the hangar to attempt my sabotage, but there was someone working on it. Armed with a pair of cutters I went to the other helicopter and cut several looms inside it.

I'll explain what a loom is. Basically it consists of thin wires bunched in groups and they carry round the information from the cockpit, to the various parts of the helicopter. Having cut the looms I then splayed them out around the cabin so anyone could see that the helicopter would be inoperative. I then danced around saying it's dead it's dead, it's not gonna fly and started singing. *"These are bare wires and Somebody's broke your wings."* (I later discovered that both these songs were written and performed by John Mayall, although as far as I knew, a band called

Atomic Rooster performed Broken Wings) I returned the cutters to the tool case and wandered back into the line shack.

Paddy Ryan then said to me "Make sure the helicopter's ready to fly."

I wandered back outside and stood alongside the helicopter. The pilot came out, approached the helicopter and as he looked inside he saw the bare wires, turned to me and said, "Did you do this?"

"Yes." I replied.

"Come with me."

I am not certain which pilot it was, but we returned to the line shack and Paddy said, "You've caused a weekend's work for the flight!"

As I sat waiting for the naval patrol one of the aircrew said, "He's done the wrong one!"

"Sorry," I replied, "I tried to get the other one, but someone was working on it."

Davy Jones wasn't very happy and said. "You've ruined my birthday. Now I'll have to stand guard over you in cells".

As far as I can recall that never happened as whoever was on guard duty, guarded me.

One of the first people to visit me in cells was the petty officer in charge of the flight crew and he said, "Are you all right?"

"Fine thanks. Tell Davy I'm sorry if I've ruined his birthday piss up."

"Will do. You do realise what you've done."

"For sure."

"You'll probably have to spend a long time locked up. Are you prepared for that?"

"I think so."

"Good luck Smiler, you're going to need it, but I hope you get what you want."

"Thanks for coming to see me. How're Paddy and John?" He smiled, "They'll get over it."

Tony, (the chap I'd been ashore with in the States), came to see me, "Smiler, everyone's talking about what you've done! In fact they're calling it Smiler's helicopter and, you've hit all the newspapers."

In fact a reporter from the Observer wanted to see me, but the navy, on my behalf blanked him. I remember the PO on watch saying something about it, but what did I know?

"Can you do something for me Tony?"

"Sure, what?"

"I've got a ticket for the Bath Festival with Led Zepp; can you give the ticket to Ellis?"

"Sure."

I actually got quite a few visitors and someone took some pictures of me and one of my visitors was John the Bish. He'd been the padre on board HMS Eagle and said, "When I heard that there was an Eagleite in cells, I thought I'd pay you a visit. Is there anything I can do for you?"

"Thanks for coming John, but I can't think of anything I want, except the obvious."

"I realise from your docs that you're a Catholic, would you like me to send along the Catholic padre?"

"Thanks for the offer, I think I'll be all right, but I do have a question for you."

"Yes, what is that?"

"When we were on board the Eagle, you always seemed to eat in our mess, surely as you hold the rank of officer; I thought you'd dine in the officers' mess."

John smiled as he said, "Actually the food was better in your mess."

"Really, were you on board when we were up in the Arctic Circle?"

"Yes."

"Now I thought the food was better then. I used to eat from the salad bar and have ice cream. But when I returned with the SAR we used to have night flying suppers and they were pretty damn good."

"Mmm, I don't know, but I do think the food was good."

I laughed, "We had a chef in our mess and we used to moan about the food, so somehow or other, he managed to put on a spread for us. He did us proud."

"Never under estimate people. I may well pop back to see you again, but I will pray for you."

"Thanks for coming John, I do appreciate it. It's nice to know that someone cares." I paused, "I know I've done wrong, but it's the only way I could think of, to get out of the navy."

"It's a shame when everything goes wrong. I shall leave you now. I believe they call you, Smiler?" "That's right."

"Try not to be too despondent, but with a name like that, I'm sure you'll manage." He then turned and left me with the guard who said,

"No more visitors for the moment. I can see you now on *This is Your Life*."

"I suppose you'll be there will you?"

"I've got news for you pal, what you've done is massive. I hear they're going to have you court-martialled."

"But I had a word with one of my mates and he knows someone who knows the Captain and he's going to see if he can get me out."

"It's too big for that and let's be honest how often does the navy have court-martials? I'll tell you pal. Never! They will love this."

"Oh thanks for that. You, are my worst nightmare."

CHAPTER THIRTY TWO

I'd been locked up for a few days when the PO on duty said, "Would you like a book to read?"

"Yes please."

"Right, we may as well go to the library and draw out a book or two for you, otherwise with nothing to do, you might go insane."

"Would that get me out?"

"Right, if you promise not to try and escape, I'll escort you to the library."

"You are having a laugh. I'll wait and see what happens, how could I escape, you'd catch me here at the gate." I replied.

I put on my cap and we wandered across to the library. I said hardly anything to the PO, but on the way one of my friends saw me and shouted out. "All right Smiler. How's it going, have they let you out?"

"Yeah, I got fed up sitting in my cell, so I'm off to the library. I think we're off to the beach this afternoon and possibly a pint. See you in Porthleven."

"I'll buy you a pint Smiler. You're a bloody hero."

"Cheers mate."

"Shut it you!" The PO said, "I'm trying to be nice to you, but I can make it hard for you."

"What'll you do, take away my mattress? Do you know what it's like sat in that cell with nothing to do?"

"Okay, okay, I'm trying to make it easy for you by getting you some books."

"I do appreciate what you're doing, but I was only having a laugh and let's be honest, the next time I'll be out, will probably be for my court-martial."

At the library, which quite frankly I didn't even know was at the camp, I was allowed several books and among the authors I chose was Alistair Maclean. The PO looked at my choice of novels and said. "Good choice, it's not what I expected."

To which I replied, "I am not an idiot, I only did what I did, to get out. If there were another way to get out, I'd have done it. Believe me I've tried to do it legally."

I remember whilst at sea I read a commission novel, which is so called because it takes a commission, which can last a year or so, to read. The book was about a monk and I had talked to Stan about becoming a monk. It seemed to be another way out of the navy. Ok, so the sex life of a monk isn't up to much, but then my sex life wasn't up to much either. Mind you the thought of walking around all day in a blanket and praying, didn't really appeal to me. I had also read the Good Soldier Schweik and in it a soldier contracted blood poison and yes, I did think of that as another choice to get out.

Eventually an officer turned up to see me and I remembered him from my days at Portland, he was a lot better than my last boss, or even my boss at Portland. When we met he said, "I am to deal with your defence unless you would prefer another officer?"

I thought for a while and said, "Is there any chance I could have Keith Rolfe to defend me?"

"Well yes you could, but he is at Portland at present undergoing training to fly another type of helicopter. And quite frankly, I don't think he'd be too happy about being dragged back from Portland to defend you. But if that's who you would like?"

"No, you'll do. I remember you from Portland."

"Right, I have to ask this question. Do you want me to defend you; after all you can always defend yourself."

"No, I'll accept you. I made a right hash of defending myself last time."

"Good. Now the next thing is, how are you going to plead, guilty or not guilty?"

"I think it would be a bit of a waste of time pleading not guilty. So I'll plead guilty."

"Good, glad to hear that. Now the next thing is, they may well want a psychiatric report."

"I saw a shrink earlier in the year."

"Yes, that's as maybe, but the navy will commission this one. So I'll arrange for you to see the psychiatrist."

"I didn't know we had one here."

"We haven't. So you will be informed when you will see him."

I was eventually driven in a car by a wren and had two escorts to accompany me to Plymouth, to see the shrink. I wore as did my escorts and driver, my number 1 uniform. As we drove along I recognised the wren from a beach party I'd been to a few nights before I went to gaol.

"Why did you do it?" She asked and I went into the whole story after which she said, "I thought you were stupid, but now. I feel sorry for you."

"By the way," I said, "If I escape you do the time for me!" Boy did they lock the car doors really quickly.

So once again I was confronted by a shrink and one of the questions he asked was, "Are you mad?"

"Isn't that what we're here to ascertain?" I quickly replied.

I returned to Cornwall to await my trial and Tony came to see me; he'd become quite a regular visitor. "I gave Ellis your ticket to the Bath festival."

"Thanks, what'd he say?"

"He's going round telling everyone that he's got your ticket, but I don't think he'll actually go."

"At least I tried. He was the first person that sprung to mind. After all, it's only one ticket otherwise I'd've given it to Stan, but now he's got a girl and you're married. By the way as I was going to be your best man and I deserted, who did you get as a best man?"

"Some petty officer."

"So how's married life?"

"Yeah it's fine. Look Smiler, you have no idea what's happening outside. Because of what you've done, we're having a meeting with the Captain. He wants to know why you did it?"

"He could've asked me. I'd've told him that I'm pissed off. I deserted, got caught, went to DQs and still I want out! But good luck with your chat with the Captain and let me know how you get on."

"Will do. By the way, do you remember Bugsy?"

"Yeah, didn't he become a photographer?"

"Yeah and you know what, he really likes it. He's been on the Antarctic survey."

"Photography, not really something I've ever thought about. Mind you the bloke over the photographic section seemed to like his work, but I think he'd rather be out of the navy. He took a picture of me when I'd just shaved my head it was quite a laugh. I was in the shack next to his and he just called me in and took a photo of me. I was a bit like a convict and had a board in front of me with Baldy written on it. Can't remember where I put the photo."

"No, I don't know him."

"He's a right cockney."

The next time I met Tony he'd been with some others to see the captain. "How was your meeting with the captain?"

"Very good. We told him we were pissed off with the way we dress and could we wear jeans out of the camp? He was with a few officers who made notes and he said they'd look into it."

Actually I did have other visitors and some even took pictures of me and so I suppose in some way, I'd become a something of a celebrity.

CHAPTER THIRTY THREE

Boom! A cannon shot rang out across the parade ground. I stepped onto the board that had served as my bed, gripped the iron bars framing the window peered out and watched as the Admiral's Flag was raised. My heart leapt for this, was to be my day.

I stepped down onto the floor and stared out of my cell into the adjoining room of the gatehouse. It was time to put on my best uniform, for today I was to be court-martialled and finally be out of the Royal Navy.

Having dressed I eagerly stood waiting for my escort to take me to my court-martial. I was looking forward to having my badges ripped off. So together with my escort, we marched to the room where the court-martial was to be held.

Quite frankly it was rather boring there were a few officers assembled along a desk, and the whole affair was presided over by an admiral and one of the officer's said, "Naval airman Bryson, do you plead guilty or not guilty to wilful damage to a helicopter."

"Guilty." I replied.

The officers looked at each other and someone said, "There's a very good psychiatric report."

The officers left the room and I sat in silence waiting for their verdict. When they returned I had to stand and hear my sentence, which their spokes person read out.

"We duly sentence you, to one year's detention."

I was then hustled out of the room and the officer who'd defended me said, "How do you feel?"

"All right."

"But you haven't got what you wanted. They have just given you one year's detention; there is nothing about you being dismissed from the navy."

I was shaken and my ashen face probably said it all and for once I really didn't know what to say but the officer said, "Is there anything that I can do for you?"

"What happens now?"

"You will be taken as soon as possible to DQs in Portsmouth."

"Okay, there is something that you can do for me. I'd like to see Naval Airman Vickers before I go. I want to give him all my money."

"Are you sure?"

"Positive sir and thank you for your help."

The officer left and I was escorted into the regulator's office and shortly Tony Vickers turned up. "What's happened Smiler?"

"I've got one year's detention, but I'm not being thrown out. So I've got something that I'd like you to have."

"Sure what is it?"

I put my hand in my pocket and pulled out all my money. (I would add here that whilst I was in cells I had no money or any possessions but before the trial I was given everything back.) "Have this I won't need it where I'm going. Shall we say it's a belated wedding present?"

"Thanks Smiler. I'll tell the boys."

"If I don't see you again, then some way or other, I got out."

"Good luck Smiler." Having said that he pocketed the money and left the regulators office.

One of the regulators said, "I could've done with that money."

"You, are the last person that I would give it to!"

The Master at Arms then called me into his office.

"Yes chief."

"What do you mean by calling me Chief I, am a Master at Arms and should be called Master."

"Oh really, I thought that there was an Admiralty Instruction stating that Master at Arms could now be referred to as, chief."

"Well I don't know where you heard that. Now this is what will happen. You are to be taken, along with your kit to Plymouth and from there; you will be taken to DQs in Portsmouth. You've been there before, so you know the routine."

I remained silent.

"Did you hear me?"

"Yes."

Yes what?"

"Yes I heard you." I replied.

Before he could have another go at me a leading regulator said, "Car and escort's here for the prisoner Master."

"Get him out of my sight." Ordered the Master at Arms On the drive to Plymouth one of the escorts's said, "Did you get your ticket?"

"No."

"How long did you get, 90 days?"

"Nowhere near it. I got a year in detention and after that, I'll still be in the navy."

"Shit man, that means you'll have to do an extra year in the navy."

"If I were you, I'd lock the doors because I really don't want to spend a year inside and if I escape you, do my time."

They soon locked the doors and one of the escorts said, "I think I'd kill myself."

"Well I'm not exactly over the moon about it. I could do the year if only I knew at the end of it, I'd be out. But this." I paused, "And you know what?"

"What?" They all enquired.

"I cannot recommend a court martial at all. In the films they rip your badges off, but they never did that to me."

"Ah but you have no rank." The wren driver said, adding, "I don't envy you doing a year."

"Look sweetheart, if you're not doing anything tonight, I've got a cosy little room in Portsmouth."

"Oh really, when I get back from Plymouth I'm finished for the day and I will be off to see my boyfriend."

"So you wouldn't like a quickie on the back seat with the hero of HMS Seahawk?"

"Tempting as the offer is, what would the two escorts do?" "Obvious really, stand guard."

"What kind of girl do you think I am?"

"Well it's obvious that you're not that easy. But think of me, no women for a whole bloody year."

"That's your problem." She replied in a huff.

"So how many are there to a cell in DQs?" One of the escorts asked.

"One, I will be alone."

"Holy shit! You'll get bored out of your brain." The escort replied.

"Having been there before I can only assume that in my spare time, I'll either be plaiting this bloody bit of rope, or else cleaning my woodwork and tin gear or reading the bible. That, is all there is to do."

"Rather you than me. I don't think I'll be deserting." Both of the escorts replied.

The rest of the journey was uneventful, but the wren driver and two male escorts looked pleased when they handed me over at Plymouth. *I wonder if they shagged her on the way back to Cornwall?*

I was once again locked up until the escort arrived from Portsmouth. When they arrived, the escort and driver who took me to Portsmouth said nothing, they didn't even say much to each other and at RNDQs, they just handed me over.

So there I was back in DQs and every name it has been given is so right for the place, The Big House, over the wall, but for me, it was a place of broken dreams. Yes, I'd done wrong, but if they'd have let me out last time, then I wouldn't have wrecked a helicopter. I thought about it, if I was good then I should get the maximum remission of one third of my sentence, which meant that I'd only serve eight months, instead of a year, and then what? I wanted to leave the navy not carry on. What a mess I was in and as I'd been told in the preceding year, I now wore a green band round my belt. Yes I was most assuredly one of those *'green cunts.'* The chief looked at me and said, "Get changed into your number eight's and hand over any valuables. Then stow your number 1s in your kit bag. You won't be needing them for a while."

My biggest problem was to get on with my life in DQs after that, I would have to seriously think about. Whatever happened I still didn't want to be in the navy, what they'd done to me may well have been a deterrent to others who no longer wished to be in the navy but for people like me, who wanted out, they, would always find a way. And yes I had tried everything else, I'd apply to purchase my way out, well my parents applied for me, but the navy wouldn't let me. Goodness only knows why I was no good to them.

For me the worst was over and that was the court-martial up until then I knew that I would get out of the navy, but now what? Should I hit the commander at DQs? Nothing sprang to mind but having already been to DQs I was used to it and knew the score, plus, having learned to deal with the situation of being alone I knew it would hold me in good stead.

CHAPTER THIRTY FOUR

So there I was back in DQs and back in the same old routine of running downstairs to grab my razor and shave, followed by running round the parade ground and then going over the assault course and finally lining up under the colonnade and numbering, followed by mail and any notices. Then it was off to breakfast and whereas the last time I'd attended lessons or did drill, this time all I did was odd jobs around the place or marched around. In my break I still had to plait that awful hemp and also had to polish the metal stairs, plus clean my tin gear and woodwork. And this time I actually managed to finish reading the entire bible, last time I'd only read the New Testament and I must say the last bit, John's Revelation was like some hippy trip.

After a few weeks the GIs actually opened a cupboard that held books and what did I draw out? Stoker RN, a story about a man who'd been in the navy as a stoker, was I insane or what? But knowing that I was in for a long time I wondered what job I would actually end up with? I had a choice of three, working in the galley for the chief cook, working for Sweeney Todd, the barber come mat maker or assisting the Commander. The job I wanted was as the assistant cook. After all it would keep me out of my room for most of the time and keep me busy.

Every so often the commander would inspect us and he referred to the letters that I'd written in which I'd stated, '*Having hit the newspapers, I must be rather famous and also, how often does the navy court-martial anyone?*'

The commander said, "You think you're famous, rather infamous I should have thought. And to state that at the age of eighteen you didn't know what you were doing, otherwise you wouldn't have joined the navy. Don't you realise that people of the age of eighteen will get the vote soon."

I remained silent and the commander also added, "Your tin gear and woodwork are not very satisfactory." He then mumbled something into a tape recorder and wandered off to the next cell.

But in all this mire one day something funny happened. It was early in the morning we'd already had the usual run around the parade ground and were lined up and told to number, which we did. But when we got to the end of the line and stopped a voice from above shouted out a number and we all fell about laughing. For that we had to double around the parade ground again. It was worth it, to get a bit of humour in that hole was brilliant.

This voice from above was obviously not God, it was a sailor who'd been locked in solitary and was trying his utmost to get out of the navy. I hope he managed it because for one brief moment he made a lot people happy.

On the sadder side one rating tried to hang himself. Fortunately he failed and once I was out of the navy we met, (but more of that later). There was also a rating who when summoned to the commander's office tried to hit him. I don't know if he got out but he deserved to.

Another little bonus of being in DQs for so long was that I became an alter boy. This was very good as I could have a quick sip of wine, although it did go through me rather quickly. As I said before I was a lapsed Roman Catholic, but if I didn't go to church then I would've stayed locked up all day Sunday. I was also thinking about Christmas and this would be my second consecutive Christmas in DQs. That was something I was not looking forward to.

One day as the Chief GI read out the notices he stated, "Admiralty Instructions have now deigned that you may grow your sideburns longer and so even here in DQs we have adhered to this and you may all grow your sideburns to the base of your ear. But this doesn't mean, we want any crab ladders does it?"

I must add that all naval ratings entering DQs have to be clean-shaven, so if they enter with a beard then it has to be shaved off. Although I would presume this was done before the rating arrived at DQs.

It occurred to me that I might have had something to do with the longer sideburns. After all Tony had said he was having a meeting with the Captain of Culdrose and asked why they were disenchanted with the navy. Could the longer sideburns have been the outcome of all this, which was sparked off by my sabotaging a helicopter? I do know this whenever I see a naval rating with long sideburns I think to myself, *'I helped to get you those.'* The irony of it is that I cannot grow long sideburns.

Now apart from the Chief GIs the highest grade in DQs was a stage man. These ratings wore white gaiters and were one of the three assistants I mentioned before. I had already been promoted as an assistant stage man, which meant I had to do more cleaning duties and one day whilst cleaning the stairs one of the ratings was telling me that he was going out.

I asked, "Will you be back?"

"Of course."

"Well I'll still be here, so which cell would you like?"

He pointed one out and I replied, "Good choice, I'll keep that one for you."

I also came across a mechanician apprentice and I asked him, about Ian whom I'd met in training?"

"Yes, he's the chief mech apprentice."

"Wow, he's done well. I joined up with him. If you see him when you get back, tell him that you met Smiler. Send him my regards and tell him that I'm trying to get out of the navy, it's not really my cup of tea, and I chose the wrong path."

"I'll do that for you."

One day as I was going about my cleaning duties the Chief Cook had a word with me, his voice was a cross between Melvyn Rose and Derek Nimmo and he said. "I saw your parents on the television last night. They seem quite sensible."

My parents had gone on television saying that had the navy released me after I'd deserted, then I would never have sabotaged a helicopter. As for the GIs, they just thought I was an idiot and deserved everything I got. In fact some of them said I had the longest sentence that they'd ever known. Others added I could have killed someone through my misdemeanour. On that count I knew that nobody would get killed. After all the helicopter never even took off, but I left the GIs in their ignorance.

One GI said to me, "Would you like to go and work on that helicopter?"

"Yes, it'd be better than being in here."

"That's right, and then you could sabotage it again!"

I said nothing. I'd proved my point the navy wasn't for me, I just wanted to leave and having tried everything else, sabotage seemed the only way out albeit a drastic way.

Another time a sailor said to me, "I had a wank in my cell."

"Blimey, you must be fit I'm knackered after that early morning run around."

"Dunno really, I just think I needed to do it, but being knackered wasn't my worry. As I was about to come my fat, I was scared in case it went over my woodwork or tin gear."

I stopped working and just laughed. As far as I was concerned this bloke was a hero.

One morning having spent about sixty days in DQs doing general cleaning duties, the commander and his entourage were inspecting me when he said, "Naval Airman Bryson, you've finally settled down and so it is that from Monday, you will be promoted to stage man. You will return your gaiters and be issued with white gaiters and you will move rooms. You will now be on the ground floor. Your job will be to assist the cook and so, your room will only be locked of a night. Plus once a month, on a Sunday you will be allowed visitors. When you have been a stage man for a while you will be allowed ashore on a Saturday, but should you come back drunk, you will lose all your remission. Do you understand?"

"Yes sir."

"And make sure that you leave your room in good order."

"Yes sir."

"Your work in the galley will start from today and on Monday you will be shown your new room and issued with white gaiters."

The commander then mumbled something into his tape recorder and wandered off.

At last I was going to be promoted to a stage man. As one usually gets a third off for good behaviour then even a ninety day man would not have to go through the crap that I went through and after sixty days, he would've been out of the place, not just starting as a stage man in the galley.

I was over the moon and so far it was the pinnacle of my naval career. To be honest I had been assisting the chief cook and stage man in the galley, for a few days. It really was the best job, plus the chief cook was a friendly bloke and quite chatty, also there were going to be days out to look forward to.

My first morning as a galley assistant was brilliant. I was having a shower and washing my clothes and talking like there was no tomorrow to the stage man about Jimi Hendrix and Led Zeppelin. Life in DQs is rather like being a monk, no sex and very little talking.

The chief cook said that his son wanted to join the navy. The stage man and I gave him an odd look.

"Just because you two don't like it, it's served me well, plus by being here, I get to serve longer in the navy and don't have to rely on my pension."

The stage man and I said nothing; well what could we say.

CHAPTER THIRTY FIVE

My first day as a stage man in the galley was brilliant; the stage man helping the chief cook had gone. Where to who knows, perhaps he'd learned his lesson and would make a good sailor, but to be a stage man he had to have been in for sixty or ninety days and from my experience I don't somehow think he'd take to the navy.

The chief was quite friendly and said, "I've seen quite a few ratings in here and quite frankly, you seem all right. I think once you get out, you'll do all right."

As a stage man with a cell on the ground floor it was often used as a showpiece and here's the odd bit. One day I returned from the galley to find that my stool was placed upside down on my bed. When I looked at it I could see why. It was filthy! To think that my woodwork had been so much better than this when I was just a *'green cunt'*, and been told that it wasn't up to the standards required but I suppose now that I was a stage man, it was over looked. Mind you I cleaned the tin gear and woodwork in my room until everything sparkled. No way did I want to go back down to being a *'green cunt'*.

I hadn't been a stage man for long, when news arrived that Jimi Hendrix had died and one of the Chief GIs said to a few of us, "I hear that they're playing Jimi Hendrix on the radio tonight. Don't think much of him myself, but I'm on duty tonight, so I'll leave the radio in my car on so that you can hear it. After all it's you lot that are keeping me in a job."

It was all just hot air as I never heard any music that night.

About a week or so later on a Sunday afternoon, I wandered across the parade ground and entered a room where my Mum and Dad were seated. In the back of the room was a marine, he was also one of the staff and said nothing. My mother said, "Your father and I are still trying to get you out of the navy. We've written to the local MP and we've been on telly."

I replied, "I appreciate what you're doing for me and I have some good news for you. I will eventually be let out for the day in Portsmouth."

"Your father and I will come and see you, but as we've said all along, if they'd let you out when you'd deserted, then this would never have happened."

I'm not certain of how long my parents were there for, but it certainly broke up the day.

On Monday it was back to normal and I noticed in the new entry was a sailor I knew from my days at Portland and I said to him, "I thought you liked the navy?"

"I used to like it Smiler, but I met a girl and I no longer want to be in the navy. What about yourself, I thought that you liked the navy and what do you do here?"

"Can't say that I have ever really liked the navy." I paused to gather my thoughts, "Well no, that's wrong. In the beginning it seemed like a game until that is, I reached Portland. Then reality hit me, I just thought things would get better but they didn't and then I got put on 737 squadron and hence to Culdrose and the Eagle where I realised my dreams were just an illusion. So I deserted, went abroad and realised that's what I should've done in the first place just hitch around, but I came back to jolly old England where I was caught, sent back to sea and when the Eagle ended its tour everyone disembarked from the ship and I was back at Culdrose, where I wrecked a helicopter and so, here I am."

"So that was you was it? We read about it and wondered who it was. When do you get out?"

"That's the problem; I merely got sentenced to one year's detention and then presumably, back in the navy."

"How come you can just wander about in here?" He asked.

"I'm a bit like a trustee. I've been in here over two months and now I help the cook."

"Two months in this place and you say you have to do a year. If you're still smiling after that, it'll be a miracle."

"I know, the most people ever serve in here is ninety days and with a third off for good behaviour, I'd be out of here now but with a year, no way. Still I suppose being a stage man is not all that bad as long as you get a good job, which I have. Oh by the way, that's why I have white gaiters and no colour thing on my belt and I don't have to make those awful mats. Also I have a cell on the ground floor which is hardly ever locked, plus I work most of the time, so I don't have time to think about what's happening." I heard footsteps approaching, "It looks as if there's someone coming, so I'll have to go. If I don't see you back at Portland then I finally got out, must go, otherwise I could be back in the ranks, so to speak."

"Yeah, I know what you mean. Good luck Smiler."

Then one day I was asked to see the commander and so I accompanied his stage man to the office. I stood there looking at the commander upon the dais with the Master at Arms by his side; I wondered what on earth I'd done wrong. Could it be that I was no longer going to be a stage man? "You asked to see me sir?" I scarily enquired.

"Yes, I have some good news for you. Your sentence has been confirmed and you are to be released from the navy. As we cannot do anything with you, this means that you will be released by Christmas but, if one word of this gets out, then I will make sure that you serve the rest of your time. Do I make myself clear?"

"Yes sir."

"Carry on in the galley and remember what I said."

"Yes sir."

I left the commander's office feeling elated. My parents' work had not been in vain plus I would most certainly not be in DQs for another Christmas. I desperately wanted to tell everyone, but, I couldn't and so I said nothing, not even to the chief cook, whom I'd got on very well with. If anyone asked why I was happy I merely replied, "Being a stage man in DQs ain't that bad, ok so shore leave's not so good but I don't smoke, my job ain't bad. I may well be in prison, but I'm alive and who knows what'll happen next?"

About a week or so later I was once again called in to see the commander; he was stood behind the dais and was flanked by the Master at Arms and the Chief GI.

"You wished to see me sir." I eagerly asked, thinking that I was to be thrown out there and then from the navy.

"Yes that's correct. Now as I stated before your sentence has been confirmed and you are, on completion of your sentence to be discharged, Services No Longer Required, from the Navy. You are to be transferred from this day hence to MCTC in Colchester, where you will serve out the rest of your sentence. Do you understand?"

"Yes sir." I replied, although I would like to have added, '*You lying bastard.*'

"Chief, accompany Naval Airman Bryson to his room where he will collect his belongings, then take him to the cage where he is to stow his eights into his kitbag and change into his number ones to await for the escort to take him to MCTC."

"Very good sir." He replied and we sauntered over to my cell, collected the few items I had left and collected my kit bag from the cage, changed, put the eights into my kitbag and marched to the gate where

I waited for my escort. I was scared stiff, I had no idea about MCTC apart from the rumour that a soldier had been doubled to death. To be honest in DQs, life had become easy, almost a doddle. No more mat making nor doubling round the parade ground as I was in the galley busy assisting in the preparation of the breakfasts, but then would my position as a stage man in DQs be taken into consideration. My silent thoughts were broken as the Chief GI said, "Naval Airman Bryson grab your kit, the transport's here to take you to MCTC."

I picked up my kitbag and followed the Chief to the huge gate that had barred my exit to the world twice, but now I would leave it behind forever. Outside the gate was a car with a leading regulator stood by the side. He looked at the Chief GI and said,

"We'll take him from here Chief."

"You'll need these it's his naval docs." The chief said as he handed over a large envelope.

"Thank you chief." He looked at me and as the chief went back inside DQs the leading regulator opened the boot of the car and said to me, "Right Bryson, put your kit in the boot, and then get into the rear of the car."

I did as I was told and the other leading regulator opened the rear door and I got into the car. Ok so I was finally going to get out, but I was scared stiff of MCTC and would I still be the equivalent of a stage man at MCTC? As for the journey, neither of the regulators said anything to me, they just wondered what the soldiers were referred to in MCTC. In the end they settled for sergeant.

CHAPTER THIRTY SIX

As we approached MCTC (Military Corrective Training Centre) in Colchester my worst nightmare was confirmed. It reminded me of the prison in *The Great Escape*. It was surrounded by wire and sentry boxes, but at least the sentry boxes weren't in towers above the wire and the soldiers had no guns.

I got out of the car and was handed over at the gatehouse of MCTC to the military provosts and the regulators drove back to Portsmouth. No doubt it was a nice trip out for them and they probably thought that I was stupid.

All three services were represented at MCTC and all NCOs had to be referred to by their rank. Most of the army sergeants were staff sergeants, they were rather rotund and wore pullovers over which was a belt which bit into their large bellies. The air force had flight sergeants and a chief represented the navy and marines. I was marched to D Wing, not as I thought, at the double. I believed everything would be done in that manner but I later discovered a soldier was doubled to death and the sergeant that did this, was on D Wing. Apparently in days gone by, the soldiers were doubling around the parade ground and one soldier complained of pains. He later collapsed and, so rumour has it, died.

The D, in D Wing stood for discharge. Because once everyone in that wing had served their time, they'd be discharged from the armed forces, albeit rather ignominiously. As for my room, I was now billeted in a Nissen hut along with other blokes who were also being discharged from the armed forces. In the winter a central stove, that burned coal or coke, supplied the heat in the Nissen hut and every morning the fire had to be dropped and the stove blackened.

I was shown into a hut and given a bed and box. Also whenever anyone new arrived they would probably find their razor blades would be depleted. How I got my razor blades in the first place I could not remember. Fortunately I am not very hirsute and any old blade did for me. I spoke to my hut mates and discovered there were three sections of D Wing and I was in part one where all newcomers were billeted. Once used to the system, we would then be placed in part two. For those that had shown the error of their ways, there was a stage man version of MCTC, but I never got that far.

Part one was a fairly lenient section. I later discovered the staff sergeants didn't check us for PA. Up until then PA to me had always been what bands used and stood for personal amplification but at MCTC, PA stood for prohibited articles.

Once again I was wearing my aircraft rigging shoes, mainly because naval shoes and boots had leather soles, whereas my rigging shoes had steel toecaps and rubber soles and were more durable. My kit had to be laid out in a wooden box and my bed was laid out according to army regulations. This meant where my pillow was, my blankets and pillows had to be boxed. It was a wonder I didn't get put on a charge for not conforming to army regulations. This was my first worry, having been in the navy I now had to do things the army way. The constant worry of not having laid out my kit properly was eating away at me. All of us in D Wing were to be thrown out, for whatever reason from the armed forces. So why the hell would we want to know how to do things the army way?

The first thing we did when we were unlocked of a morning was to fall in outside the hut and march down to the washhouse.

The good thing about MCTC was that I could now talk to other people and was able to draw books out from a library. For every meal I was with others and the army gave us three meals and a supper. These consisted of a breakfast of porridge and a fry up and one Scotsman used to put salt on his porridge. There was also a midday meal and an evening meal and once we were locked up there was supper, which consisted of soup and bread.

In RNDQs ratings that smoked were allowed one cigarette a day, which was at lunch break, whereas in MCTC smokers were allowed two cigarettes a day. This was at lunch and with the evening meal. I was so glad I didn't smoke. I saw blokes smoking leaves and even bits of carpet.

What we didn't talk about was why were in there. In fact some soldiers didn't want to be thrown out. I met other sailors who were supposed to have mutinied but speaking to them, it was farce.

Then came the day when I was transferred to the second part of D Wing. The first thing that struck me were the beds. Oh dear, it was as if there was a box of blankets at the head of the bed. How on earth would my blankets ever look like that? Also as the weather got colder not many used the extra blankets for warmth, this meant breaking up their blanket box and remaking it again every day. I was now an old lag and was about to get firsthand experience of what PA was.

One of the staff sergeants came into the mess in the evening and said, "I'm looking for PA," and asked a couple of blokes to tip. This entailed tipping out the contents of their box and bedding. The staff sergeant was looking for tobacco. This was another thing that worried me, would I be asked to tip? Fortunately it never happened to me.

Once I was established in the mess I got along quite well. One bloke wrote home to say he had to make his blankets look like a television, which was about right. Another didn't know what to say and so I said, "It's dark when we get up and it's dark when we go to bed. What happens in between? I can't tell you about." He actually wrote it down and sent it home.

Most of the time we could attend courses, one was on car mechanics, one on woodwork and the other on painting and decorating. There were also other odd jobs to do around the place and one sailor said to me, "I was with this squaddy (soldier) and he asked me to burn the rubber off the electric cable. He wanted to sell the copper and I said no way. That's what I'm in here for!"

After we'd done our day's work and eaten, there was nothing to do. So in our hut we decided to try and make a Monopoly board. We could get the board from the woodwork class and reckoned together we would be able to figure out what there was on the board. Someone on the painting course could paint it, as for the dice, back again to the woodwork class. The problem was the cards, so we gave up the idea. Even if we had made a Monopoly board, we'd probably have got nicked for having PA. We were not allowed any games, perhaps they thought we'd gamble. But they couldn't stop gambling. That year Colchester played Leeds in a cup-tie; I bet that Leeds would win. I lost my cocoa on that as Colchester actually beat Leeds.

Apart from more cigarettes and being billeted with others I was also able to write more letters and so wrote to my friends. Tony wrote back and one day when I was in the RSM's office. I looked at an old jam jar almost full of water, where he placed his used cigarette ends. He said to me, "I see one of your friends wishes he could do what you did to get out of the navy."

"I told him not to do it, sir." "I know."

I told this to the others in my mess and they said that he wasn't supposed to refer to anything we wrote in our letters.

One night as I looked into my soup, I said to the others, "Ere there's maggots in my soup."

"Complain then!" Someone said.

I shouted out of the window until a staff sergeant appeared and said, "Yes Bryson."

"I want to make a complaint, staff."

"What about?"

"There are maggots in my soup." I then thrust my mug out of the window to show him.

"Does anyone else in this hut wish to complain?" He said.

So several other members also complained about maggots in their soup and we thought we'd hear no more about it. But that weekend as we were all stood on parade the RSM said. "I hear there have been complaints about weevils in the soup. They are perfectly all right to eat."

What a bastard, I thought. *What's his last name Bligh? It's like HMS Bounty all over again. I wonder how he would feel as he was dished up weevils with his Sunday roast? But I thought weevils were something that Bo Diddley sang about.*

I was now able to receive visitors every month and my parents with either one of my brothers or another of my relatives came to see me on visiting Sunday.

As I had to put on my number one uniform mum said I looked better, as for my younger brother Gerry he said, "Do you go up to the wire and look at the people outside?"

Mum also said, "My father, as you know, was from Spain in the Basque Country. He joined the navy and deserted."

I thought she'd said this to make me feel better, as dad had grown his sideburns longer presumably for the same reason. As for my grandfather I have since discovered he did join the royal navy as a diver. I have been reliably informed since then that he came home on leave and went through the front door, closely followed by two policemen. Whereby my grandfather went out of the back door and was never seen again. Rumours have it he returned to Spain. After the visits we were all strip searched, looking for tobacco.

After one visit one of the sailors said to me, "I met your dad in the toilet and he asked me if I wanted a puff of his fag. Your dad's all right."

That sailor was lucky enough to be released for Christmas, as I also thought I'd be released for Christmas 1970, but no. I spent my second consecutive Christmas locked up.

CHAPTER THIRTY SEVEN

I met a tank driver and a gunner. The gunner said they could drive the gun along and I asked, "What's the difference between a gun and a tank?"

"You live in a tank," He replied.

There was a time when someone had been caught with a tattoo on their arm of MCTC; this led to everyone in the wing being strip searched. Two sergeants entered the hut and we were told to strip and stood there naked as they looked for tattoos. What happened if they had any tattoos of MCTC? They went sick, what happened I later found out by firsthand experience. No I didn't have a tattoo; in fact I have no tattoos on my body at all.

It was when I was working in the cookhouse and took a pack of butter. I also asked another bloke to take some. The idea being we would be able to spread the butter on the bread we received of a night with the soup, which was now maggot free.

We were marching along to our hut when we were stopped and had to turn and face the huts. The staff sergeant said, "Someone has stolen some butter from the cookhouse. You have stolen other men's rations. So would the person, or persons, who stole the butter, come out to the front. If you don't, you will all be thoroughly strip searched."

I went forward and handed over the packet of butter, as did the soldier. The staff sergeant said, "Go sick in the morning you two."

The following morning we were both on sick parade and went in front of the medical orderly who said, "How do you feel?"

"Fine."

The two of us were sent to see the major who said, "Do you realise what you did? Depriving a man of his rations is a deplorable thing. Have you anything to say in your defence?"

"No, sir."

"Fourteen days restricted diets and one day's loss of remission. Remission has to be earned; it is not something that is automatically given. Do you understand?"

"Yes, sir."

Whilst on restricted diets I was seated away from the main group, along with others on restricted diets. The diet as far as I can remember, consisted of soup for lunch and evening meal and of an evening all I was allowed was cocoa. It was this that I lost as a bet when Colchester beat Leeds in a cup-tie match. During the time I was on restricted diets, I could only do light duties.

One day a sailor was told off for wearing shoes. It was because his shoes had leather soles and all sailors were then issued with DMS (duty moulded sole) boots. As I had my aircraft rigging shoes, I thought I might be able to still wear my shoes and put in a request to see the major.

My request to wear shoes was denied and so I went along to Liklak, to draw my boots. Liklak the store man had got his name because of the way he drilled us. Normally sergeants would cry out, left right, left right, left. But not Liklak. It was always, Lik lak, lik lak, lik lak, lik! Hence his name of Liklak.

There was now a problem with my shoes. They had to be on display and the toe caps had to shine so I could see my face in them. I looked at them in a forlorn manner. The toes were scuffed and I wondered how on earth I would get a shine on them, let alone spit and polish them.

My hut mates helped me out, I explained why I was looking so dismal and so they set about shining my shoes and I never wore them. They were kept under a duster shining away.

One day, whilst walking around D Wing, a soldier and I saluted each other and we were both given a bollocking by a staff sergeant. How bizarre, we were only having a laugh. Which believe me, in that place was very hard to do.

I mentioned earlier attending classes and some of them I did again, otherwise there were very few things to do and it avoided doing the crap jobs around the camp. I helped build a sentry box; and it was while I was in the woodwork class a soldier said about his life on the run.

"I was working on a building site and this bloke was saying about this woman in the next town, whose husband was in the army. Anyway, she was looking for a shag." He paused adding, "That bastard was fucking my wife, and we had a fight. I got caught and that's why I'm here."

There was one soldier who'd spent so long out of the army he'd forgotten everything about it. Why they put him in MCTC is a mystery to me. They should have just let him carry on instead of sending him to military prison. There was also a marine who wore a black beret instead of the usual green beret and so I said, "Where's your green beret?"

"I never got past the initial training," he replied

Another time I was working with a soldier and he said, "Swing the lamps and tell us a sea story."

One day I returned to my hut from the library with two books and one of my hut mates said, "What books did you get, Smiler?"

"Wizard of Oz and Pinocchio."

He looked at his copy of Bleak House and said, "Maybe, Smiler, you have the right idea."

"I just wanted something jolly to read and take me away from this crap hole."

THE WRONG PATH

One night as we were gathered around the stove, a soldier was kicking the lid on and off and I said, "Don't do that mate it's getting on my nerves."

With that I got head butted.

"Sorry about that, Smiler. I didn't mean to do it you're a nice guy."

"Apology accepted. It's this place. It gets to you."

"What are you going to do when you leave here, Smiler?" Another soldier said to get things back to normal.

"Do what I joined the navy for—just travel. What about you?"

"Well you may have a lot of memories, but you'll have nothing to show for it. Me, I'm going to get married. Have an electrical business a house and kids. At least I'll have something to show for it."

"It's not for me. I deserted and went on the run in Sweden and Holland and realised then, that's what I should've done. Instead of joining the navy, hitch around and not have to worry about the police pulling me in as a deserter. Bliss, pure bliss."

"But you may get killed out there on the road."

"I didn't get killed last time and anyway it'll be an adventure, no one telling me when to get my hair cut or what to do each day."

I thought the comment about me getting killed whilst I hitched around was odd, as being in the forces, had war broken out any one of us could've been maimed or killed.

None of us wanted to be there although some of the soldiers said if there were a war they'd sign up.

Of a Sunday morning I also attended church, again it was to get me out of the hut. On Christmas Day prior to going to church a soldier said to me. "Smiler, you're about my size. How about swapping uniforms?"

"I might as well; after all I've now learnt how to do the things in the army fashion."

So we swapped as did another sailor and soldier, but they got nabbed. This was because the soldier had a moustache and sailors don't have moustaches. They were made to change back again but one of the staff sergeants looked at me and said. "There's something wrong here, but I can't quite understand it."

Christmas dinner 1970 was so much better than the previous year and the staff sergeants served us. One of the soldiers had been in a similar situation to me. He agreed it was better than last year and 1971 would finally bring about my release from the royal navy.

Plus on Boxing Day we were allowed to watch Top of the Pops and they showed Jimi Hendrix. I just freaked out.

As the weather became colder we were issued with army great coats, but the only thing was they had no buttons on them. So we were issued with buttons to sew on ourselves. I sewed mine on down one side and one of my hut mates said, "Smiler, are you short of buttons?"

"No."

"Well you're supposed to sew them down both sides. You'll get done for it."

The following morning as we stood on parade in our great coats a staff sergeant approached me and said, "Bryson, why is there only one row of buttons on your great coat?"

"Well I'm only doing it up one way, staff."

"The next time you're on parade, you will have two rows of buttons sewn on. Do you understand Bryson?"

"Yes, staff."

"Because if you don't. You'll be on a charge."

One morning towards the end of my time at MCTC, I pointed up to a light in the washhouse and said to the staff sergeant, "Excuse me, staff, but the light bulb's not working."

"You're a little ray of sunshine. You get up there."

Being in D Wing towards the end of our time we were allowed to go on working parties. This meant going outside the camp to army barracks and carry out odd jobs. It was a pleasant change. One soldier was never allowed on outside working parties and when I asked why he said, "I've escaped before."

About a week or so prior to release I went to see the Camp Commandant, who said,

"And what do you hope to do upon your release from the navy?"
"Become a recording engineer, sir."

This idea of mine was brought about by someone saying they'd worked in a recording studio. How true it was is another thing, but it sounded like a good idea.

There seemed to be more gay soldiers than gay sailors. In fact there was one soldier when asked by the Camp Commandant what he was going to do when he was out of the army said, "Flog my arse."

My day of release finally arrived and like all the others, I shouted out my name out of the window. It was the final act of defiance. Apparently one could be held back for doing this, but nobody ever was.

So on the 13th March 1971 together with a few others I was marched out of D Wing for the last time. I changed into my civvies, handed in my ID card and was given money and a piece of paper, stating I was no longer in the navy and was now able to take up employment.

I caught the train to Liverpool Street and with the others we went into Dirty Dick's pub and down into the basement. Upon the wall were masses of stamps. We stuck a stamp on the wall and all signed it. That first pint felt so good, as did freedom.

I got home and my parents were so glad to see me. Mum said, "The World in Action team wanted to send a car to pick you up. I said no, as I'm not sure of how the army would take it. The World in Action team will be round later on in the week to interview you, as will the Hampstead and Highgate local paper."

I was so glad to be out of the navy and to celebrate I played a record, which was Crossroads by Cream.

I told the World in Action team the name of the rating that tried to hang himself. They brought him up to London so we could meet. It was just so good to see him. If you read this, you know who you are and I hope all is well with you and your family.

One of the soldiers knew I was into music and told me to look him up when I was out. I went round to his flat and he said, "Would you like to be a roady for the Robert Stigwood Association?"

I thought this would be a brilliant idea and said, "Yes." To which he replied, "You have to sleep with me first." Needless to say I declined the offer and went home.

EPILOGUE

So there I was finally out of the navy and boy was I glad to be out, but what happened to my life? Firstly I took a job as a delivery driver and when asked what I'd done, I replied, "I've been in the royal navy."

It was fine except that one man asked to see my naval documents and when he noticed I'd been court-martailled and sent to DQs and MCTC, he sacked me. Not a very good start to my life in Civvy Street.

I mentioned about a car from the people at World in Action, coming to pick me up. World in Action did a programme about people who were disenchanted with life in the forces and they arranged for me to meet the sailor who'd tried to hang himself. We were out and it felt great!

As a consequence of what I'd been through in MCTC, for years afterwards I had nightmares about the place and believe me, it has not been easy writing about the place. In fact many years later there was a programme on the television about MCTC. I watched it for a while and then turned it off. I couldn't go through all that again.

In hindsight RNDQs the naval prison was based on solitude and fitness and is now no longer used, but MCTC was based on correcting people for military life and worrying them, at least in D Wing, about being searched for cigarettes, or not doing things in the army manner, for me it was a living nightmare.

On the good side, I met Stan and his girlfriend Jane, together with Pop at a pub in Ealing. We sat outside and all felt glad to be out, although Jane was not very happy with Stan. I'll explain, in Stan's words.

"It was getting near to Christmas and Jane and I had very little money and so I bought a xylophone. You understand, Smiler and anyway, I learned to play jingle bells on it."

Yes I did understand, perhaps being in the navy had made all of us irresponsible children. I did ask about Ellis, but nobody knew what had happened to him, or if in fact his name really was Ellis. Stan also said that Tony Vickers was still in the navy, but he wanted to leave.

I did meet Tony several years later on a train coming back from the West Country, my girlfriend's sister lived there. Tony was still in the navy and had grown a beard.

"Hallo Tony," I said, "how're you?"

"Smiler, I've just been telling this lot about your helicopter."

"Tony, tell them not to do it, there must be better ways to leave the navy.

I also met Jake Fordham; he was one of the leading hands who'd named me ugliest bloke of the year. I went into a pub with my girlfriend at Earls Court and Jake served me.

"These are on me, so how are you Smiler? I'll come and have a drink with you."

Jake was the manger of the pub and said, "When the Royal Tournament is on, you should come down for a drink with the Field Gun Crews."

Jake also told me about another rating who got his ticket, but he worked it in a much better method than I had. As for the Field Gun Crews, as much as I admired them, I never went back for a drink.

THE WRONG PATH

I also met Ricky at the Boat Show one year. He was one of the sailors doing a demo on life saving or something from a helicopter. We went for a drink and he was either a petty officer or a chief, either way, he was telling the fish-heads how to dive!

I also met some of the soldiers I'd been in MCTC with; I met the one who I'd changed clothes with, the one that I'd saluted and a Scotsman.

As you've probably gathered, some of the sailors did well for themselves, as for leaving the navy, I believe now the chances of a sailor going to war are pretty high, therefore anyone thinking of joining any of the armed forces should think seriously of the consequences.

Let's be honest here, had the captain of the Eagle when he spoke to me after I'd just got out of DQs said to me, "Right, I can understand your dislike of the navy, it's not everybody's cup of tea, but just see this commission out and when you return to HMS Seahawk with the SAR, then instead of putting in for another ship, you will be dismissed from the navy."

Now that I could gladly have done, in fact I did do it.

I cannot justify what I did to get out of the royal navy. As for me, I have more than paid my dues, I did my time and the nightmares were awful, and as for actually becoming a record producer, or even travelling abroad. That as they say, is indeed another story, but the ironic part was later telling people about what I'd done to get out of the navy. I used to tell them about my confrontation with the commander and commodore. They thought it was funny and would then tell their friends. So it's because of them I have decided to put all this down in print. But most of the time, I said nothing as I was terrified of what the repercussions would be, plus as I've said, I wasn't proud of what I'd done, in fact I felt like a criminal.

Having just left the navy I required a reference for a job and so I asked an old school friend's dad to give me a reference, he declined and I think it was because in the Second World War, he'd been a sergeant.

From that day hence, there has always a stigma attached to what I'd done and so for many years I told no one about it.

Finally, as for the blokes I met in RNDQs and MCTC, I have deliberately not mentioned their names, but I wish you all well, wherever you are.

I suppose in hindsight, the good thing about being in the navy, is the camaraderie, which is sadly lacking in civilian life, but then being out of the navy is it freedom? Oddly enough some of the jobs I've had since leaving the navy and believe me, there are many, still have their rules and regulations and to keep changing jobs is not something I would recommend.

I've also discovered rather late in life I am an artist, so who knows, perhaps I should've become an entertainer. Mind you over the years I have been described as a comedian, but for myself I've become more of a raconteur.

WRONG PATH BACK PAGE INFO
PHIL R BRYSON

This is far from being a gung ho story as it begins with me waiting to be tried by court martial, which in the early 1970s was unheard of.

When my story begins, I am in Hendon and about to move to Basildon, the reason being my parents' house was to be pulled down to make way for the M1.

Once in school at Basildon, I am given the name of Smiler which naturally carries on when I join the navy.

Prior to that I became a mod, I really enjoyed riding my scooter and listening to RnB and soul music and also seeing a few bands. In fact my local band at the Mecca Dancehall in Basildon was the Dave Clark Five.

Naturally this all ended once I joined the royal navy but upon being recruited I was talked out of being an aircraft mechanic into being an electrical mechanician apprentice. I also had to serve twelve years instead of nine years and three in reserve. I agreed as I was informed that I would become a petty officer, which is the equivalent of a sergeant.

Needless to say, I failed as a mechanician and transferred to become an aircraft mechanic. In this I excelled and came second in the class and was once again up for super promotion, provided I gained the right qualifications once working on aircraft. As I wanted to work on helicopters, I ended up in Portland working on a Wasp helicopter. I was over the moon as this helicopter went on board a frigate, not an aircraft carrier.

One thing led to another and once I was qualified to work on a Wasp helicopter I then decided to do various courses to enable me to get promoted to a leading hand, the equivalent of a corporal. I was done for walking through the dockyard with my hands in my pockets. This meant stoppage of leave and extra duties for ten days. I would add here that Portland was a real gem of a place for weekend leave as it is virtually shut down at 3pm on a Friday.

I got friendly with a few blokes and we ended up chatting up some Swedish girls and got passports as we intended to see them in Sweden. Also I became twenty which in those days I was allowed my first tot of rum, I had what is known as a magic glass, in that it never emptied and hence I got drunk and was thrown into cells. My birthday was on a Friday and I was so annoyed as I'd missed seeing John Mayall's Bluesbreakers in a pub near to Southend. Although when I did get home on Saturday I saw Peter Green's Fleetwood Mac.

I treated the navy as a joke and some of the officers were far from happy about how I addressed them. The navy really wasn't for me.

Eventually I got transferred onto maintaining a Wessex helicopter and also I had been trying to further my education by taking more GCEs all that ended as I had to work on the helicopter.

Then disaster happened, I was transferred to RNAS Culdrose in Cornwall, this was the end for me as I could now envisage going on board an aircraft carrier.

All was not in vain as I met a couple of blokes and we used to go to Falmouth and go to a pub and sometimes on to a party.

I was right as I was sent on board HMS Eagle, the second largest aircraft carrier in the navy plus I was to be misemployed as Captain of the Heads, which basically meant I was a toilet cleaner. After six weeks at sea I was transferred to the S.A.R. once again on H.M.S. Eagle.

It was a small ships flight and the ship sailed to America, it was 1969 and the year of Woodstock, which if I'd known about I would have deserted and gone to see it. Instead when the ship returned to the UK I went home on summer leave, after which I never returned to the ship, I caught a train to Sweden. Oh how glad I was that I'd got a passport a few years earlier. I chose Sweden as it was the time of the war in Vietnam and I thought I would be able to live there.

It was not so, instead I bought a Swedish sleeping bag and high pack and someone sold me a tent. I then hitched to Amsterdam in Holland where I worked as a dishwasher. Not much of a job but I did get a wage rise then went back to Sweden this time I went tot Stockholm, previously I'd been to Gothenberg.

I ended up trying to sell encyclopaedias all to no avail but help came in the form of an Englishman whom I went to Gothenberg with and stayed with him, his wife and baby and I got a job as a window cleaner, once again I got a pay rise. I decided to return to England for Christmas as the Swedish have fish for Christmas dinner and I am not too keen on fish.

As I left the boat at Tilbury I was caught and back in the navy and I was sent to naval prison, although I did talk my way out of 28 days into 41 days in RNDQs, naval prison.

In 1970 I was once again on the S.A.R. on HMS Eagle, the captain of the ship saw me and I told him that I would desert again. My mess mates said I was a liability and should be thrown off the ship.

In the end I wrecked a helicopter and was duly sentenced to one year in naval prison. What I did hit a lot of newspapers and eventually I did get thrown out of the navy.

After being thrown out of the navy World in Action did a programme about naval prison and I helped the researchers get in touch with a chap who'd tried to commit suicide in naval prison. Nowadays **all** the armed forces give the people the option of giving a year's notice to leave. It would appear that what I and others have done has made a difference to the armed forces.

Inspiration

I was inspired to write this story as I'd told people snippets of it and they thought it was funny. I've also given talks and the people wanted to hear more, in fact whenever I've talked to anyone about my life in the navy, they want to read the book.

Takes place

The story takes place in the mid to late 1960's. I travel around various naval bases and also served on two ships, one was an RFA; these are used to refuel royal navy ships.

Plus there is the hitching around Europe, navy and military prison.

Main characters

Here there is a problem as I am the main character. As I was in the navy things change, it's not like being in a regiment as sailors only serve so long on one particular ship.

Yes there are other characters but they come and go as the story changes.

Why I think it will appeal to readers and target audience

Firstly as I've mentioned there are the people I've spoken to also it will appeal to other members of the armed forces because they will hopefully, see the funny side of things that I do, also they will like the way I am insubordinate to some officers that I do not like.

If I start doing talks I would sell more books. Plus radio would allow me to do snippets from the book and in that way promote it.

PERSONAL INFO

Bio

As I've already stated this book about the five years I spent in the navy. I am now retired but in my life as a youth my parents were always moving.

    I started work as a telecommunications apprentice, but as I wanted to travel, I joined the navy. At the time I was a mod, which I enjoyed as it was a way of life, the way I dressed, the music, everything. I actually wanted to be a DJ.

    In the navy I did have a go at being a DJ, since then I've broadcast on hospital radio, which is like a small radio station, and I've also done mobile discos.

    After the navy I hitched round Europe and saw everything I could think of seeing in the way of tourist sites, from Rome to the Acropolis in Athens, to walking along the banks of the Danube, and both sides of the Berlin wall.

    The following year I hitched up to Scandinavia and saw the Midnight Sun, I ended up being a landscape gardener, saw the Rolling Stones with Mick Taylor on guitar and then hitched to Greece, then island hopped to Cyprus, where I took a plane to Israel where I had the time of my life on a kibbutz. I was even asked to be in a play. Upon returning to England, I became a telephone engineer, and then I left to become a photographer.

    I've also been a dispatch rider and a van delivery man. I've had more jobs than I care to remember.

Finally This is my first book.

www.ingramcontent.com/pod-product-compliance
Lightning Source LLC
Chambersburg PA
CBHW030109100526
44591CB00009B/341